Essays
on the
Heidelberg Catechism

Wipf and Stock Publishers
199 W 8th Ave, Suite 3
Eugene, OR 97401

Essays on the Heidelberg Catechism
By Thompson, Bard and Berkhof, Hendrikus
ISBN 13: 978-1-4982-9792-9
Publication date 4/28/2016
Previously published by United Church Press, 1963

The window illustrated in the front cover design is located in Santee Chapel of the Lancaster Theological Seminary. It honors three men closely associated with the writing of *The Heidelberg Catechism*—Zacharias Ursinus, Caspar Olevianus, and Elector Frederick III.

BARD THOMPSON
HENDRIKUS BERKHOF
EDUARD SCHWEIZER
HOWARD G. HAGEMAN

Essays on the Heidelberg Catechism

WIPF & STOCK · Eugene, Oregon

Contents

Foreword	5
BARD THOMPSON	
1. Historical Background of the Catechism	8
2. The Reformed Church in the Palatinate	31
3. The Catechism and the Mercersburg Theology	53
HENDRIKUS BERKHOF	
4. The Catechism in Historical Context	76
5. The Catechism as an Expression of Our Faith	93
EDUARD SCHWEIZER	
6. Scripture and Tradition: The Problem	124
7. Scripture and Tradition: An Answer	139
HOWARD G. HAGEMAN	
8. The Catechism in Christian Nurture	158
Authors' Notes	181

Foreword

Most of the essays contained in this volume were delivered as lectures at the Annual Convocation of Lancaster Theological Seminary in January 1963. The Lancaster convocation marked the opening on this side of the Atlantic of the celebration of the 400th anniversary of the Heidelberg Catechism. At about the same time a similar celebration was being held at the University of Heidelberg in Germany, the home of the Catechism.

The celebration at Lancaster had its origin in a suggestion made in 1959 by James E. Wagner, who was then Co-President of the United Church of Christ. It was made possible by a special grant from the General Council of the former Evangelical and Reformed Church.

Special guests for the convocation were the members of the North American Area Council of the Alliance of the Reformed Churches throughout the World Holding the Presbyterian Order. The Council, which had sponsored the new Miller-Osterhaven translation of the Heidelberg Catechism, held its annual meeting in conjunction with the celebration.

It is our hope that through this book the distinguished writers will make a significant contribution from the Reformed perspective to the continuing discussion of the nature of tradition in the life of the church.

Authors' notes appear at the back of the book.

ROBERT V. MOSS, JR.

Office of the President
Lancaster Theological Seminary
Lancaster, Pennsylvania

Bard Thompson

•

HISTORICAL BACKGROUND OF THE CATECHISM

THE REFORMED CHURCH IN THE PALATINATE

THE CATECHISM AND THE MERCERSBURG THEOLOGY

BARD THOMPSON is professor of Church History at Lancaster Theological Seminary.

CHAPTER ONE

Historical Background of the Catechism

WHEN MARTIN LUTHER posted his notorious theses, the Palatinate was governed by Ludwig I, aptly named Pacificus, for public tranquillity was a prime consideration of his policy. While Ludwig remained placidly papist, he could not arouse himself to any particular passion against Luther. On April 26, 1518 the Wittenberg monk appeared in person at Heidelberg to defend forty propositions of the "new theology"[1] before his fellow Augustinians, who were assembled there in General Chapter. The theologians of the University of Heidelberg, though disposed to scholastic theology and a stolid loyalty to Rome, listened courteously to the Saxon upstart, and parried his thrusts with both skill and self-restraint.[2] Yet three young men in Luther's audience were captivated by his whole performance.

One was Martin Bucer, a Dominican, who had already disavowed Thomas Aquinas, his proper master, in favor of the fresh teachings of Erasmus. Luther treated him to a supper of dainties and doctrine, which proved to be the commencement of his evangelical career.[3] Another was John Brenz, a fierce but imaginative man, who would shortly carry the Lutheran teachings to Württemberg. The third was Theobald Billican, who became the Reformer of Nördlingen.

Soon the Lutheran opinions began to filter out of Heidelberg into the far reaches of the Palatinate. In 1522 when Brenz and

Historical Background of the Catechism

Billican presumed to expound the gospel in Lutheran fashion, they caused a tumult in Heidelberg and were duly silenced.[4] Elector Ludwig was not greatly edified by the Reformation and continued to abide in the papal doctrines throughout his reign.

THE REFORMATION IN THE PALATINATE

In 1544, at Ludwig's death, Frederick II succeeded to the electoral dignity.[5] Through the writings of Bucer[6] (then the distinguished Reformer of Strassburg), he had begun to acknowledge the evangelical religion; yet he cowered at the prospect of retaliation by Charles V, Holy Roman Emperor. The first Reformation decrees were delivered at the end of 1545 and the beginning of 1546. They were elicited from the reluctant Elector by certain ardent Lutherans among his political councillors; by his nephew, Duke Otto Heinrich of Pfalz-Neuburg, already a convinced Lutheran[7]; by Luther's colleague Philip Melanchthon, son of the Palatinate, alumnus of Heidelberg,[8] whose advice was solicited in the spring of 1545; and by the people themselves, who, according to an old tradition, struck up Speratus' hymn *Es ist das Heil uns kommen her,* during Advent of 1545, making the Church of the Holy Spirit in Heidelberg resound with their mandate for the Reformation.

Frederick, having already enjoyed Holy Communion in both elements at Easter of that year, permitted the custom to be used generally by an October decree; and at the opening of 1546, he sanctioned the celebration of the Lutheran "Mass" in the Church of the Holy Spirit. These initial advantages were shortly pursued by the introduction of preachers, the preparation of church manuals, and the arrival of evangelical experts, among whom Bucer himself was one.[9]

These steps were taken in 1546, the year that Luther died—which points out that the Reformation came late to the Palatinate. It came, in fact, just at the time when the influence of Melanchthon began to be challenged by the strict adherents of Luther, producing a division of parties that brought turmoil to the whole of Germany. The Church of the Palatinate was inevitably drawn into the vicissitudes of this conflict.

Frederick's decision occurred, moreover, at a critical point in German politics. In April 1547 the imperial army demolished the Protestant forces of the Schmalkaldic League at the Battle of Mühlberg. Thereupon the Emperor imposed the Augsburg Interim on Protestant lands, restoring the Roman religion virtually intact. Some defiance was shown to the Interim by the students at Heidelberg,[10] but Frederick himself had no heart to resist. By consequence of these events, the religious life of the Palatinate lapsed into a state of confusion, as the government, which had sanctioned the Reformation but timorously, now applied the Interim haphazardly. Thus the people had little security in either the old religion or the new.[11] Frederick's courage did not stiffen until Charles V had finally been brought to terms by the Peace of Augsburg in 1555. He then ventured to follow a cautious policy in favor of the Reformation, avoiding sensations. But before the old man could divine the exact mode of procedure, the pest claimed him; he died at Alzey on February 28, 1556.

It is important to note the provisions of the Peace of Augsburg. Each prince was entitled to determine which religion would prevail in his realm; but no rights whatever were extended to any except Roman Catholics and adherents of the Augsburg Confession.[12]

Otto Heinrich, who had ruled for many years as count (*Pfalzgraf*) over the Neuburg district of the Palatinate, succeeded to the electoral throne. He was decidedly Lutheran and—what is more to the point—a Lutheran politician of prime importance. After 1553 he labored to bring into reality the inner unity of Protestantism, not merely for its own sake, but as a means of dealing with the Roman Catholics. In this effort, his staunchest ally was Duke Christopher of Württemberg, to whom the problem of Protestant unity was essentially a theological problem, requiring the attention of the secular authority, as well as of the theologians. Christopher paid close attention, therefore, to the two theologians who shaped the religious policy of Württemberg—Philip Melanchthon and John Brenz, both of whom were members, at this stage, of the milder, Melanchthonian party in the Evangelical Church of Germany.

Otto Heinrich, in contrast to Christopher, found the problem to be essentially one of political unity, based upon the common adherence to the Augsburg Confession. Having less appreciation for the theological difficulties, which nevertheless became more and more critical in the German Church, Otto Heinrich was apt to see them as *Theologengezänk* (the squabble of theologians). Yet it is apparent, both by the policies which he pursued and the church order which he introduced in the Palatinate, that the Elector did not go untouched by the Melanchthonian tendency.[13]

MELANCHTHON'S INFLUENCE

What was this "tendency" ascribed to Melanchthon and his colleagues? It was, above all, *a spirit*—a spirit of charitableness, moderation, and union,[14] particularly toward the several branches of Reformation Christianity, but even in some degree toward the Roman Catholics. It was a spirit of theological wholeness, one that combined an openness to new insights from scripture with a reverence to tradition[15] and a zeal to conserve catholic unity. Beyond that, however, Melanchthon deviated from the so-called Lutheran orthodoxy at two points of doctrine: free will and the Lord's Supper.

With reference to man's freedom, he adhered closely at first to Luther's early opinion. In the *Loci Communes* of 1521 Melanchthon declared: "Seeing that all things which happen, happen necessarily according to divine predestination, there is no freedom of the will."[16] But he was deeply affected by Erasmus' polemic against Luther in the book *De Libero Arbitrio* of 1524[17]; and subsequently he began to insist that the work of conversion must be attributed to three "connected causes" *(copulationem causarum)*: the Holy Spirit as the primary agent, the Word of God as the instrumental agent, and the human will which consents to this action and freely yields to it.[18]

In contrast to Luther and to those scrupulous theologians who quoted Luther chapter and verse,[19] he denied that the divine grace is wrought upon man as upon a block of wood: so corrupt that he can only resist, so perverse that he must be converted despite himself. Such an idea seemed to defeat the meaning of preaching and to nullify the ethical personality of man.[20] For

Melanchthon, the human will is a *causa concurrens* in conversion: it decides when preaching evokes the decision; it accepts God's gift of grace freely offered. In 1558, with unusual candor, he described the viewpoint of the orthodox Lutherans as "Stoic and Manichaean" determinism, and assailed it as "contrary to the Word of God, harmful to all discipline, and blasphemous."[21]

Of far greater importance to the turn of events in the Palatinate was Melanchthon's doctrine of the Lord's Supper, which he attained only after years of worry and reflection.[22] Already by 1528 he entertained serious doubts about Luther's doctrine, particularly Luther's treatment of ubiquity and the Real Presence.[23] Yet in all matters of uncertain exegesis, Melanchthon adhered to the testimony of the ancient Fathers, which appeared to sustain Luther in this instance.[24] So he remained at Luther's side through the stormy era of the Marburg Colloquy, and afterward at the Augsburg Diet (1530). Thus, in the Augsburg Confession, Melanchthon taught that the body and blood of Christ are "truly present" *(vere adsint)*—the German addition adding "under the form of bread and wine"—and are "distributed" *(distribuantur)* to those that eat.[25]

Later in 1530, however, a treatise by John Oecolampadius convinced him that the Fathers did not in fact support Luther[26]; and that piece of intelligence proved to be of critical importance. "I am not willing to be the author or advocate of a new dogma in the church," Melanchthon informed Brenz. "We must take care not to confound the doctrine of the ancients."[27] By 1534,[28] his thought having crystallized, Melanchthon concurred generally with the doctrine of the Spiritual Real Presence[29] which John Calvin and Martin Bucer also affirmed. Calvin himself appreciated the firmness of this accord.[30]

As Melanchthon understood it, the center of Eucharistic theology was neither the Zwinglian memorialism, on the one hand, nor the tactual eating of the chemical matter of Christ's body, on the other hand, but a real life-union of the *person* of Christ *(vivi Christi, totius Christi)* and the soul of man—a life-union which is neither figurative, nor moral, nor merely by efficacy, but real and substantial.[31] Melanchthon expressed this idea in a formula which is found many times in his writings,[32] and appears as

Historical Background of the Catechism

follows in Otto Heinrich's Palatinate Church Order of 1556:

> What is administered and received in the Lord's Supper?
>
> The true body and blood of our Lord Jesus Christ. For the Lord Jesus Christ has instituted this nourishment in order to attest that he wills to be truly and really with us, and to live in the converted, communicating his benefits to them, and be effective in them.[33]

Similarly in the *Loci* of 1535, Melanchthon taught:

> When one offers the bread and wine in the Supper, there is truly offered the body and blood of Christ, and Christ is truly there, and is powerful in us, as Hilary says: This eating and drinking "makes it" that Christ is in us and we in him.[34]

While he did not doubt that a "sacramental union" occurred in the Lord's Supper,[35] Melanchthon admitted no possibility of a local inclusion: the body and blood of Christ are not attached to the elements or mixed with them.[36] Christ is not "in the bread," much less enshrined in a pyx. On the contrary Melanchthon insisted that the sacramental presence is given "with the bread" (*cum pane*), or preferably "in the Supper" (*in coena*), and certainly "in the use" (*in usu*)—which is to say: Christ is present in our use of the sacramental action as a whole.[37]

In 1540, to "explain things better,"[38] Melanchthon took it upon himself to publish a revised edition of the Augsburg Confession in which he "improved" certain of the articles according to his own views. In the tenth article, on the Lord's Supper, he removed the words *vere adsint* (truly present); replaced the word *distribuantur* (distributed) by the less physical word *exhibeantur* (tendered); and added his preferred phrase *cum pane*. As amended, the article now taught that *with* the bread and wine, the body and blood of Christ are tendered to the communicants.[39] In Article XVIII, on free will, the confession newly declared that "spiritual righteousness is wrought in us when we are *helped* by the Holy Spirit. Moreover, we receive the Holy Spirit when we *assent* to the Word of God."[40]

As early as 1541 the Roman controversialist, John Eck, detected these and other substantial changes in the original text. But for one reason or another the Lutherans did not choose to be so tedious. For that matter, Luther persisted in lavishing praise upon the successive editions of the *Loci Communes*,[41] in which these same deviations were perfectly evident, although there were times, in fact, when his friendship for Melanchthon became strained to the breaking point.[42]

Under the guise of being the latest, improved edition, Melanchthon's amended text of the Augsburg Confession, called the *Augustana Variata*, won its way into churches and schools, and became the basis of theological discourse at diets and colloquies, never to be seriously challenged until 1561. And as late as 1580 the signers of the Formula of Concord complained: "It is no longer clear to us or to our theologians what is the confession once offered to the Emperor at Augsburg."[43]

After the death of Luther (1546), however, Melanchthon's stance came under fierce attack by certain pugnacious conservatives in the German Church who referred to themselves as Gnesio-Lutherans, "genuine Lutherans." They swore by the letter of Luther; classified Zurich and Geneva, as well as Rome, with the rabble of Antichrist; and detected something highly "ungenuine" in the Melanchthonian opinions. Beginning in 1549 Flacius Illyricus, the known leader of the conservative party, assailed Melanchthon for his attempt to live with the Leipzig Interim by explaining its Roman features as *adiaphora*, nonessential matters.[44] Subsequently in 1552 Joachim Westphal decided to reopen the old and bitter feud concerning the Lord's Supper. On behalf of the Gnesio-Lutherans he denounced the satanic blasphemies of Calvin, aiming indirectly at the Melanchthonians. Everyone who doubted the corporeal presence, and literal eating of Christ's body belonged to the ranks of the heretics as perverters of Luther's doctrine and Word of God. By clear implication, Melanchthon was consigned to that category.

Calvin undertook to reply to Westphal, not once, but three times; and in the last of these rejoinders he claimed to agree with the Eucharistic theology of the Augsburg Confession as Melanchthon interpreted it.[45] This was an unfortunate stroke on Calvin's part, for it openly established the connection between Calvin and Melanchthon and illustrated the growing influence of Reformed theology in Germany. Thereafter the Gnesio-Lutherans attempted

Historical Background of the Catechism

to stigmatize the Melanchthonians by calling them Crypto-Calvinists. With astonishing bitterness this controversy swept over Germany at the very time that Elector Otto Heinrich attempted to reorder the ecclesiastical affairs of the Palatinate.

THE NEW CHURCH ORDER

At the heart of the Elector's reforms was a church order which he put in force in 1556 and which purported to be a faithful expression of the Augsburg Confession. But which version of the Augsburg Confession did it represent? The two oldest church historians of the Palatinate, Henry Alting and B. G. Struve, gave conflicting answers to that question. Alting insisted that Otto Heinrich's manual represented the *Variata,* while Struve maintained that it was faithful to the 1530 original.[46] Among the modern commentators, Barbara Kurze, for one, seems to decide with Struve.[47] Yet Struve was unaware of the real source of this church order. It was, in fact, a reproduction of Otto Heinrich's Neuburg *kirchenordnung* of 1554, which was, in turn, strongly dependent upon John Brenz's Württemberg manual of 1553.[48] There is reason to believe that, in this period, the Württemberg theologian Brenz and his prince, Duke Christopher, were amenable to the Melanchthonian opinions.[49] It is clear, at least, that their Eucharistic doctrine required the expression *cum pane*[50]—a formula which was now brought over to the Palatinate.[51] Moreover one must weigh the significant fact that Melanchthon's own *Examen Ordinandorum*[52]—a compend of theology for the clergy—was incorporated into the Palatinate Church Order of 1556, including his statement on the Spiritual Real Presence. Thus the answer to the question is almost certainly the *Variata.*

There was another important part of the heritage from Württemberg. From Brenz's church order the Palatinate acquired one of the least liturgical types of Lutheran worship,[53] in which the church year was curtailed, the word priest uniformly replaced by "minister" *(kirchendiener),* the use of Mass vestments discouraged, and in which a fairly heavy emphasis fell upon preaching and instruction.[54] In accord with this new liturgical policy, Otto Heinrich required the churches of the Palatinate to be purged of images, crucifixes, side altars, and such. Exorcism was forbidden in baptism, and the Elevation of the Host specifically proscribed.[55] This radical reduction of the cultus would shortly make it possible for the Palatinate to undergo a further transition to Calvinist worship in the subsequent reign of Frederick III.

In these efforts Otto Heinrich was assisted chiefly by Michael Diller, his court preacher, who participated in the irenic spirit of the Melanchthonians, and by Johann Marbach, on leave from Strassburg, who was inclined toward the more rigid Lutheranism. Marbach, having undertaken the organization of the Evangelical Church of the Palatinate, received the Elector's bid to become General Superintendent[56]; but when the Strassburg authorities demurred, the office was given instead to Heinrich Stoll, a respected Heidelberg preacher of Melanchthonian sympathies, who, however, died in 1557.

CONFLICTS AT HEIDELBERG

Meanwhile the Elector had another earnest concern: to invigorate the University of Heidelberg, making it a spiritual and intellectual center for the diffusion of Lutheran doctrine.[57] If Struve is correct,[58] there were but two professors in the theological faculty—one of them an avowed papist with a concubine—whose instructions were attended by a small and torpid body of students.

In the fall of 1557 Melanchthon came to Heidelberg, at the Elector's invitation, in order to view the moribund university and prescribe for its recovery.[59] While the new constitution specified the Augsburg Confession as the basis of doctrine, the magnanimous Elector apparently believed that the Melanchthonian spirit required an openness to all shades of Protestant theology, even Reformed theology—or else, as Barbara Kurze suggests,[60] he was simply naïve in his expectation that Lutherans, Melanchthonians, Zwinglians, and Calvinists could work together in perfect harmony.

Thus in 1557 the divinity faculty was furnished with a young French Calvinist of commanding ability, Pierre Bouquin (Petrus Boquinus). Shortly after, owing to woeful misinformation on Melanchthon's part,[61] Tilemann Hesshus was called to Stoll's post as General Superintendent and "first" professor of the theological faculty. Presently he revealed himself to be scrupulously Lutheran,

Historical Background of the Catechism

exuberant in his advocacy of Gnesio-Lutheranism. Calvin observed that he was the sort of fellow who thought he could prostrate his opponents simply by breathing on them.[62]

Hesshus claimed that the consecrated bread *is* the body of Christ, which is received corporeally by the mouth; yet he clothed this doctrine with subtle qualifications which Calvin found difficult to fasten down.[63] (For the same reason, Theodore Beza referred to him as "the syllogizing ass.") He spent his time assailing Calvinists and Crypto-Calvinists for trifling with the Word of God and for teaching what he insisted to be a symbolic conception of the Supper.

In 1558 Thomas Erastus was called to Heidelberg as court physician and professor of medicine in the university. A Swiss, Erastus had been trained in both theology and medicine, and with considerable zeal defended the Zwinglian view of the Eucharist.[64] Having been appointed to the Consistory, he took a bold stand against Hesshus and contrived to bring more men of the Swiss persuasion into the theological faculty. And so, in an age that ascribed no particular virtue to the idea of toleration, Otto Heinrich ventured to surround himself with a most peculiar collection of churchmen: Gnesio-Lutherans, Melanchthonians, Calvinists, Zwinglians. This theological hodgepodge teetered insecurely upon the basis of the *Variata,* for the Peace of Augsburg awarded no religious rights save to Roman Catholics and to Lutherans who espoused the Augsburg Confession.

Either in 1558, toward the end of Otto Heinrich's life, or, as Hans Rott suggests,[65] immediately after his death, the almost inevitable tumult broke out in Heidelberg. The *Theologengezänk* of which he had spoken lightly, overwhelmed his own city. The Elector, being childless, decided to leave a monument to his memory in the venerable Church of the Holy Spirit. It was an ornate piece of statuary, depicting cherubs and virgins in various stages of undress; and it was erected in the choir of the church, exactly where communicants received the Lord's Supper. Hesshus had approved the monument with delight, knowing that it would surely affront the Reformed theologians who prized simplicity. Presently the *diaconus* at the church, William Klebitz, whose sympathies were decidedly Reformed and decidedly hostile to the naughty statue, took up the cudgels against Hesshus, and a great fight commenced.[66]

Hesshus pressed the attack in other ways. He would allow only Luther's hymns to be sung, and thwarted the Elector's plan to prepare a union hymnal, including the compositions of Bucer and Melanchthon.[67] He attempted to establish Luther's Catechism in opposition to all others[68]—a matter which he apparently deemed to be critical inasmuch as so many Protestant refugees had been allowed to enter the Palatinate, each with his own confession.[69] Suddenly, in February 1559, Otto Heinrich died.

Frederick III,[70] called the Pious, who now came to the electoral throne, had been reared strictly in the Roman faith, but under the persuasion of his wife—Princess Maria of Brandenburg-Bayreuth—had publicly professed the Augsburg faith in 1546. Frederick suffered somewhat under family management. His wife was vigilant lest he be seduced by Calvinism. And as he ascended the throne he received an earnest admonition from his son-in-law, John Frederick of Saxony, to disinfect the Palatinate of the "devil's manure" (namely, Calvinism). Yet there is hardly any doubt at all that the Augsburg Confession which the new Elector affirmed was the *Variata* of Melanchthon. In fact one of the major points of his ecclesiastical policy was the unity of all Protestants in view of the Roman resurgence being manifested by the Council of Trent.

For months Hesshus had been provoking trouble in trifling ways, such as having a napkin held under the Host lest some particles drop to the floor. In April of 1559, while Hesshus was away, Klebitz presented seven theses on the Eucharist to obtain from the university a bachelor's degree in theology.[71] After the fashion of Calvin, he interpreted the "communion of Christ's body and blood" in terms of receiving the "vivifying virtue" of Christ's life. When Hesshus returned and discovered that the Reformed upstart had been given a degree by a supposedly Lutheran university, he railed against Klebitz from the pulpit, using every choice epithet at his command. Through the summer of 1559 the controversy raged, in the course of which Hesshus threatened his opponents with excommunication and (if the legend reported by Struve is true) attempted to snatch the communion chalice from Klebitz's hand.[72]

Historical Background of the Catechism

His patience utterly exhausted, Frederick summoned the clergy to his presence early in September and demanded that peace be restored by common adherence to the tenth article of the Augsburg Confession. But which Augsburg Confession? Hesshus said the body of Christ is "in" the bread. Some of his disciples said "under" the bread. Others of his disciples said "in, with, and under" the bread—to which one exuberant follower added: "round and round" the bread.[73] The Calvinists and Melanchthonians, under common pressure from Hesshus, had united on the formula of the *Variata:* the body of Christ is received "with" the bread.

On September 10, presumably at the Elector's instruction, Diller made a public announcement that peace had been found in the Augsburg Confession and that all parties would now abide by the formula "with the bread." That was the very interpretation which Hesshus could not tolerate. In monumental wrath, he exposed the differences between the two Augsburg Confessions and declared that Article X of the *Variata* was so ambiguous that "Christ and the devil could hide under it together."[74] Klebitz, equally enraged, proceeded to carry on the battle by physical violence. Presently Frederick found it necessary to dismiss both warriors and promptly dispatched his secretary to Wittenberg to ask for Melanchthon's counsel.

Melanchthon's *Responsio*,[75] dated November 1, advised Frederick to lay aside all formulae and rely strictly on the Pauline theme that the bread which we break is "the communion of the body of Christ":

> The word κοινωνια needs to be explained. It does not mean that the nature of the bread is changed, as the papists say. It does not mean that the bread is the substantial [*substantiale*] body of Christ, as the theologians of Bremen say. It does not mean that the bread is the true [*verum*] body of Christ, as Hesshus says. But it means κοινωνιαν, that is, a communion by which union [*consociatio*] takes place with the body of Christ—a union which takes place in the use [*in usu:* Melanchthon means that the grace of the sacrament is personal, a personal communion with Christ, and cannot be realized merely by the consecration of the elements] and not without our cognizance, as when mice nibble at bread. . . . The Son of God is

truly present in the service of the gospel, and is truly effectual in those who believe [*in credentibus*]. And he is present not for the sake of the bread [*propter panem:* Melanchthon was severely critical of what he called the "bread worship" of the Gnesio-Lutherans] but for the sake of men, as indeed he says: "Abide in me, and I in you." And again: "I am in the Father, and you are in me, and I in you." And in this true comfort he makes us members of himself and certifies that he will vivify our bodies.

There is, perhaps, no more decisive statement than this of Melanchthon's view of the Lord's Supper—and none more congenial to the Reformed doctrine. Frederick received the *Responsio* as a definitive statement.[76] Yet there is ample evidence to believe that the Elector was basing his policies neither upon a docile subservience to Melanchthon, nor upon the letter of the Augsburg Confession, but upon the Scriptures, to which he now devoted himself in conscientious study. This attitude was itself a principle of Reformed theology, which uniformly insisted that only the Word of God can prescribe for the church. Promptly, Frederick reorganized the Consistory into a committee of six—three theologians, three learned politicians—and put at its head the brilliant young Wenceslaus Zuleger, who had mastered his Calvinism in Geneva itself.[77]

REPERCUSSIONS

These developments in the Palatinate caused profound repercussions in Germany. The first occurred in Württemberg where Brenz had been fretful for some time over the ambiguity of Article X in the *Variata*.[78] In 1559 that respected theologian—next to Melanchthon in prominence among the Germans—took up Luther's doctrine of ubiquity, undergirded it with a peculiar Christology, and thereby asserted the real presence of Christ, received by the mouth, even by the unworthy. At the Synod of Stuttgart in December 1559, Württemberg subscribed to the entire purport of this teaching[79]; and for the first time the doctrine of ubiquity was written into a Lutheran creed.[80]

Melanchthon grieved over Brenz's defection,[81] and longed to be delivered "from the rage of the theologians" (*a rabie theo-*

logorum). That deliverance came to him in the form of death on April 19, 1560. Meanwhile Frederick's family conspired to keep him Lutheran. In June, John Frederick of Saxony appeared in Heidelberg to attend a family wedding. It occurred to him to bring along two contentious theologians, Maximilian Mörlin and Johann Stössel,[82] who succeeded by their impertinence in promoting a public debate on June 3. In the course of the next five days, Pierre Bouquin defended the seven Calvinistic theses which Klebitz had presented in his heyday.[83] On behalf of Gnesio-Lutheranism, Mörlin and Stössel responded with twenty-four prickly propositions, the gist of which is found in the following[84]:

> 1. That the true body and blood of our Lord Jesus Christ is truly and substantially present, dispensed, and exhibited, in, with, or under the bread and wine. . . .
>
> 4. That . . . [Christ] is thus received and eaten not merely in a spiritual fashion by faith, but also bodily [*corporaliter*] by mouth, according to the sacramental conjunction of body and blood with bread and wine. . . .
>
> 7. That . . . the body and blood of Christ are received not alone by the pious and worthy, but also by the godless, hypocrites, and unworthy; yet with this distinction: that . . . to the pious such eating is salvific, while to the godless it contributes to greater damnation and judgment.

In the long Latin debate, Bouquin defended the Calvinist doctrines so convincingly that Frederick, already patient of Calvinism, ventured to consider its full adoption.[85]

Meanwhile the unfolding defection of the Palatinate continued to ignite the Gnesio-Lutherans. From Bremen, Hesshus pronounced solemn judgment on the apostasy of the Elector, which was reechoed by Brenz, Westphal, and the rest. Bouquin answered Hesshus treatise for treatise, and Calvin penned his final tract against that "incorrigible bull."

In the midst of this alarm the Lutheran princes assembled at Naumburg in January 1561,[86] to recapture their sense of solidarity against the resurgence of Romanism. Fully conscious of the division in Lutheranism, and disheartened by the seeming apostasy of the Palatinate, the princes resolved to renew their subscription to the Augsburg Confession. But which Confession? Elector Frederick III stoutly insisted upon the *Variata*, claiming that it was a faithful representation of the original statement, "but also explained it more fully."[87] The Gnesio-Lutherans, however, proceeded to expose the Melanchthonian heresies in the *Variata;* and they demanded subscription to the original document, together with the Schmalkald Articles.

In the end a dubious compromise was worked out by Elector Augustus of Saxony, whose sympathies were apparently with Frederick. Accordingly the princes signed the Confession of 1531 as the point of evangelical unity, yet acknowledged the *Variata* as an authentic interpretation of the Augsburg faith.[88]

The meaning of the Naumburg Colloquy was profound. For the first time it brought the validity of the *Variata* into open question. And despite the compromise, it left the contending parties in the German Church more hopelessly divided than before. Duke John Frederick of Saxony, who had stalked out of the colloquy in disgust at the compromise, now presented himself as the soul of opposition against each and every deviate of the unaltered Confession (including his own father-in-law); and in this effort he was soon joined by an increasing number of princes.

In view of this isolation, Frederick III resolved to lift the Palatinate Church above the bewildering pressures of Gnesio-Lutheranism, and, with the help of Calvinist theologians, to erect a church catholic and reformed, faithful as far as humanly possible to the Scriptures. He repeatedly denied that he had any formal knowledge of Calvinism[89]; and whether or not that assertion was actually true, it represented his deliberate intention to found a church which transcended theological partisanship and which appealed to no perishable authorities. (Yet Frederick was visited by Beza in 1559; Calvin dedicated a commentary to him; Henry Bullinger sent him letters of counsel.) The Elector, however, refused to sunder the deep, emotional ties which bound the Palatinate to the traditions of the evangelical church of Germany; never as long as he lived did he fail to affirm the Augsburg Confession (which is to say, the *Variata*) as a correct interpretation of scripture and the ultimate bond to German Protestantism.

In need of new leaders, Frederick decided to invite more Cal-

Historical Background of the Catechism

vinists to Heidelberg and to permit the Lutheran remnant to disappear through resignation or dismissal. Caspar Olevianus[90] was already at his post. Like Calvin, Olevianus had studied law at Orléans and Bourges. Presently he found himself drawn into the circle of the Reformed congregations which flourished secretly in those towns; and in this fashion he became convinced of Calvinism. Around 1557, having just taken his doctorate in civil law, he submitted to the instructions of several Reformed divines. Calvin, to whom he was particularly indebted, encouraged him to attempt the preaching of the gospel in Trier, his native city, which happened to be the seat of one of the preeminent archdioceses of Germany. There he labored at great odds for several months in 1559, until the archbishop set upon him with a small army and bound him over for punishment and, likely, execution. But through the vigorous intervention of Frederick III, whose son Olevianus had once tried to save from drowning, he was released and brought straightway to Heidelberg, where, after a brief tenure in the chair of dogmatics, he took the more congenial post of pastor in the city. At thirty-four he was not as accomplished as Bouquin; nor would he match the massive learning of Zacharias Ursinus.

In the months following the Naumburg Colloquy, Heidelberg was furnished with other Reformed theologians, notably, Peter Dathenus,[91] a Flemish Calvinist, who was appointed court preacher; Immanuel Tremellius,[92] one-time professor at Cambridge, who became the Hebraist of the university; and Zacharias Ursinus. Thus the entire theological faculty consisted of Calvinists: Bouquin in New Testament; Tremellius in Old Testament; Olevianus in dogmatics, shortly to be succeeded by Ursinus.

After Naumburg the Elector also required a severe overhaul of Christian worship, according to Reformed principles. Altars were replaced by communion tables; the Host, by ordinary bread; the golden communionware, by ruder utensils. Pictures were whitewashed, statues covered, organs closed. Latin choral music was abolished, and German hymns appointed for congregational singing. The church year was purged of all saint days and reduced to the major Christian festivals.[93]

ZACHARIAS URSINUS

Finally in the summer of 1561 Frederick took the decisive step of inviting to Heidelberg a Reformed theologian whose stature was scarcely less than that of Calvin himself: Peter Martyr, who was then in Zurich. Of him Calvin wrote: "The whole [doctrine of the Eucharist] was crowned by Peter Martyr, who left nothing more to be done."[94] Martyr declined the invitation, owing to his advanced years, but he had a brilliant German pupil named Ursinus, whom he recommended for the post.

Thus, in the fall of 1561 Zacharias Ursinus, aged twenty-seven, assumed his duties at Heidelberg. His appointment was exceedingly propitious, for he represented in his own person the whole intellectual development which the Church of the Palatinate had undergone. The foundations of his theology had been laid by Melanchthon, with whom he had lived and studied for seven years at Wittenberg, and upon whom he lavished praise: "When Philip has spoken, I cannot and dare not think otherwise."[95] In 1557 he took leave of his master and toured the great centers of Reformed theology, including Zurich, to which he was strongly attached, and Geneva, where Calvin received him kindly. Through Melanchthon's influence (and not despite it) he found himself drawn into an intellectual union with the great Reformed divines, notably Calvin, Bullinger, and Martyr.

Ursinus commenced his career in Breslau, his native city, as a teacher in the Elizabeth's School; and there he employed Melanchthon's *Examen Ordinandorum* as the basis of his religious teaching.[96] The Gnesio-Lutherans accused him of being a Crypto-Calvinist. He defended himself by publishing 123 theses on Christian doctrine,[97] which evoked Melanchthon's warmest praise,[98] yet betrayed a certain drift toward the main currents of Reformed theology, especially with respect to election.

When at last Ursinus was dismissed from Breslau in 1560, his teacher Melanchthon was dead; and he decided to go to Zurich, "where there are pious, great, and learned men." There, in the city of Bullinger and Martyr, he was led decisively to Reformed theology, with Martyr as his foremost guide. On October 6, 1560 he informed a friend by letter that he was in full accord with the Zurichers *de Sacramentis, de Providentia et Electione Dei, de libero arbitrio, de Traditionibus humanis in Ecclesia, de disciplinae christianae severitate.*[99] Such was the disposition of the young theologian who assumed the chair of dogmatics in Heidelberg.

PREPARATION OF THE CATECHISM

In 1562 Elector Frederick III commissioned his theologians to prepare a catechism. His main idea, which he put so clearly in the preface to the Heidelberg Catechism,[100] was to arrive at an instrument that would establish and edify the newly conceived Church of the Palatinate "according to the pure and consistent doctrine of the holy gospel." This, he added candidly, required additional reforms if the untaught youth and older folks were to be delivered from unsound doctrine, unbiblical practices, and idle speculations, and exercised instead "in the proper and true knowledge of God." The Heidelberg Catechism was designed to put an end to the snarling partisanship of Gnesio-Lutherans versus Crypto-Calvinists and to arrive at peace and catholicity on the basis of no perishable authorities, but of God's Word alone—*das einige Fundament aller Tugenten und Gehorsams* (the only foundation of all virtue and obedience).

How was the Catechism composed? The *exact* source of the questions and answers has become a problem[101] almost as complex and unedifying as the *exact* reasons for the development of the Roman Canon. Shortly after his arrival at Heidelberg, Ursinus prepared a *Summa Theologiae* of 323 questions as the basis of his instruction in theology. Later he wrote a *Catechesis Minor* in which the substance of the *Summa* was reduced to 108 questions and most of the speculative problems were removed. And in the *Minor,* Ursinus introduced the threefold division which governed the shape of the Heidelberg Catechism: man's misery, man's deliverance, man's gratitude for deliverance. The old tradition, first proposed by Alting,[102] that Olevianus also prepared a preliminary draft, has no apparent basis in fact.

The two productions of Ursinus were turned over to a committee which included, according to Frederick's preface, "our entire theological faculty in this place, and all the superintendents, and distinguished servants of the church."[103] This must certainly mean that Bouquin, Tremellius, and Ursinus (faculty), and Olevianus, Erastus,[104] Diller, and Zierler[105] (consistory) had a share in the preparation of the final draft. These men patterned their composition after the *Catechesis Minor,* from which some ninety questions were taken over to the Heidelberg Catechism. The Elector himself kept careful watch over the proceedings,[106] and in at least one instance (Question 78) required an entire answer to be rewritten because it savored somewhat of Zwinglian memorialism.[107]

At this point, according to a long-standing tradition, the committee turned over their dry, Latin doctrines to Olevianus, who gave the Catechism its warm, devotional character as he cast it into German. The proof of this is supposed to become obvious when one compares the style of the Catechism to that of the Palatinate Liturgy and other writings by Olevianus. Walter Hollweg, however, has recently reviewed the evidence and concluded that Olevianus' consummate editorial work is decidedly improbable.[108] We have not likely heard the last of that matter.

The Catechism was formally adopted by a synod convened at Heidelberg in January 1563. On Tuesday, January 19, Elector Frederick added his preface, in which he described the new instrument as "a fixed form and model" by which ministers and schoolmasters would instruct young and old, forgoing all whimsical changes and private opinion.[109] The text underwent four editions in the course of 1563. In the second edition, apparently at Olevianus' insistence,[110] Frederick ordered the Mass to be condemned in the eightieth question; but the *full* text of that condemnation did not appear until the third edition. This action was an obvious rejoinder to Session XXII of the Council of Trent (1562) which affirmed the sacrifice of the Mass and anathematized those who said otherwise. In the fourth edition, which was brought to completion on November 15,[111] the Catechism appeared in the context of the Palatinate Church Order, which included the complete text of the new Palatinate Liturgy. And thus it became the formal standard for all doctrine, discipline, and divine worship.

The Liturgy was prepared by the same committee that was responsible for the Catechism, although Olevianus advised Bullinger of its salient features in such fashion[112] that many scholars assume he directed the liturgical work. The services were decidedly Reformed, and while some of them may have borne a special affinity to the church order of John à Lasco,[113] the Liturgy as a whole embodied the shape and the ideas which were typical of the entire Calvinist rite. Here, the Lord's Supper, couched in terms which were unmistakably Calvin's, was required "at least once a month" in the cities and towns.[114]

Could this strange creation possibly endure in the midst of Germany? To apprehend the incongruity of it all, one must hear the Lutherans singing the hymn composed in 1592:

> Guard thy saints with thy Word, O Lord,
> And smite the Calvinists with thy sword.

DEFENSE OF THE CATECHISM

The ominous signs of disaster were shortly forthcoming. On April 25, 1563 the Holy Roman Emperor acknowledged receipt of the Heidelberg Catechism and, having found it at variance with the Augsburg Confession, solemnly warned Frederick that he had exceeded the Peace of Augsburg and should count himself in jeopardy.[115] Another remonstrance followed from three neighboring princes who pronounced the sacramental doctrine of the Catechism "a seductive and damned error."[116] Frederick replied that he would not allow the words of either Luther or Calvin to be thrust against him, but only the Word of God, upon which he claimed his catechism was based. "I cannot see that such a catechism contains false or pernicious doctrines . . . unless one is prepared at the same time to condemn the Word of God itself." He denied, moreover, those "baseless charges" that he had defected from the Evangelical Church of Germany: "Again we acknowledge and embrace the same divine Word [and] the [Augsburg] Confession derived from it."[117]

The princes were not satisfied; they proposed a colloquy.[118] Frederick said that he was sick to death of the "restless theologians"[119]; but finally agreed to a debate at Maulbron in April of 1564, when the Heidelberg divines contended against those of Württemberg. An irreconcilable conflict ensued over ubiquity, leaving the parties more hopelessly divided than ever.[120] Now Frederick's enemies connived to depose him by securing some official declaration that the Palatinate had forfeited its religious rights specified only to Lutherans and Romanists in the Peace of Augsburg. With this prospect in mind, Emperor Maximilian II summoned the German Diet to meet in the spring of 1566, and rather appropriately at Augsburg.

On May 14, lacking the support of a single prince, Frederick was accused of innovations which were to be straightway abolished on penalty of exclusion from the Peace of Augsburg and personal deposition in favor of his son Ludwig. Frederick entered upon the floor of the Diet attended by another of his sons who marched in ceremoniously with the Bible and the Augsburg Confession. Said the Elector:

> What men understand by Calvinism I do not know. I can say with a pure conscience that I have never read Calvin's writings. As to the . . . Augsburg Confession that I signed at Naumburg with the other princes, the majority of whom are present today: in that faith I continue firmly, on no other ground than that I find it established in the holy Scriptures. . . . And I doubt that anyone can successfully show that I have done or accepted anything that stands opposed to that Confession. On the contrary, my own catechism is drawn word for word from divine, not human sources, as the references in the margins will prove.[121]

He was resting his whole case on the thesis that the Palatinate Church had gone beyond all perishable authorities to the Scriptures alone. In this vein he continued:

> If any person, regardless of age, station, or class, even the humblest, can teach me something better from the holy Scriptures, I will give him hearty thanks and be readily obedient to divine truth. . . . Here are the Scriptures. . . . Would it please your Imperial Majesty to do this I would take it as a great favor.

Frederick had scored a point. His old friend Augustus of Saxony exclaimed, "Fritz, you are more pious than the lot of us."[122] But the Emperor pressed for his condemnation. In the days that followed, Frederick repeatedly disclaimed all knowledge of Calvinism, repeatedly affirmed the Augsburg Confession, repeatedly

Historical Background of the Catechism

proffered the Bible so that anyone who wished to could teach him something better. But no one obliged.[123]

Toward the end of that year the rumor became current that Bullinger had ghostwritten the Heidelberg Catechism. While the Elector was not nearly as ignorant of the Reformed divines as he pretended, and had actually asked Bullinger to contribute a confession in support of the Catechism,[124] he nevertheless denounced the rumor: "The report that I had my catechism . . . prepared in Zurich by Bullinger and company is an open and barefaced lie."[125]

Meanwhile the Palatinate reform was being assailed in polemics by Brenz, Hesshus, and their partisans. Those assaults were usually answered by Ursinus in the name of the theological faculty; and seldom did he fail to cite the Melanchthonian standards in support of the Catechism.[126] The Elector persisted in the same policy. As he expected his death (which came on October 26, 1576), Frederick hastened to write a last will and testament, making his valedictory to the long, heartrending controversy.[127] In that final document of his reign he subscribed to a single norm of doctrine beyond the Scriptures. It was the Augsburg Confession.

CONCLUSIONS

What do we make of all this? Was the German Reformed Church *precisely* a Zwinglian church, as we are accustomed to say? There is least evidence of all to believe that. Was the German Reformed Church a Melanchthonian church, as the Mercersburg theologians were apt to suggest, in opposition to their low-church opponents? Surely the spirit of Melanchthon savored the whole Reformation in the Palatinate. But just as surely, the Mercersburg divines overstated their case. The Palatinate standards were undeniably Reformed, as the sacrosanct Synod of Dort acknowledged when it pronounced the Heidelberg Catechism "a most accurate compend of the orthodox Christian faith."[128]

Was Frederick III "converted to Calvinism"?—a stock question among the older experts. The question itself is too simple. Neither the political realities nor his own piety allowed the Elector to concede that the Palatinate Church had forfeited its true participation in the evangelical community of the Augsburg Confession. As the heir of Melanchthon's spirit—a spirit of peace, of theological wholeness, of catholic unity—Frederick tried to transcend the debilitating and almost idolatrous partisanship of the Gnesio-Lutherans and, with the help of Calvinist theologians, to erect a church catholic and reformed. It is the catholicity of the Heidelberg Catechism to which we point. As the voice of the historic church, it teaches, without speculation or undue partisanship, the faith commonly held by Reformed Catholicism of the sixteenth century.

CHAPTER TWO

The Reformed Church in the Palatinate

WHY A CATECHISM? What sense is there to the catechetical books of Luther or Calvin or the theologians at Heidelberg? In order to unfold the answer, we must consider three propositions of Reformation theology: (1) The Word of God presents itself as an inexhaustible resource to the believer; it cannot all be heard in one sermon, nor fathomed at one reading. (2) The believer who takes the Word seriously must become captive to it, forever remaining its pupil and disciple. (3) The true relationship between the believer and scripture is not one of private opinion, but a lifelong discipleship which gives depth and seriousness to religion and energizes the priesthood of all believers.[1]

What folly it is, said Luther, to suppose that we can "master perfectly in one hour" all there is to know about the Word of God. He had nothing but contempt for those "presumptuous saints" who, after one reading, claimed to be doctors of the scripture.[2] Nay, said Luther, in his sermon on Psalm 111:

> Whoever earnestly regards God's Word as God's Word knows very well that he will forever remain its pupil and disciple. The others master God's Word at first flight, and brashly render opinions and personal judgments on it. . . . As the fear of God is the beginning of all wisdom, so the contempt of God is the beginning of all folly.[3]

Luther meant that the believer's reception of the Word is not some sort of instantaneous infusion of truth. It is, like repentance itself, an enduring, demanding process that goes on through life. But according to Luther, such discipleship has rich rewards. For the Word which begets faith in our hearts will lead us on to "understanding," namely, it will teach us the full measure of our Christian vocation; it will instruct us more and more in our mutual priesthood to one another.[4]

Calvin was equally impressed with the inexhaustible character of God's Word. "When we come to hear the sermon or take up the Bible," he said, "we must not have the foolish arrogance of thinking we shall easily understand everything we hear or read."[5] "There is wisdom laid up there which surpasses all our senses."[6] Calvin agreed with Luther, moreover, that faith, once formed by the Word of God, places us in perpetual subjection to that Word. We become its pupils and disciples as long as we live. Never is our faith so perfect, so sure of itself, that it releases us from that happy bondage.[7]

THE PURPOSE OF THE CATECHISM

To stimulate the believer's lifelong discipleship to the Word, the Reformers resorted to the catechism. By and large the medieval catechism had been a guidebook for the priest, illustrating how he could best translate the dogmas of the church into viable language for laymen; but seldom were those books put into the hands of the parishioner for his own study. Among the first to conceive of the catechism as a lay folks' manual were the Bohemian Brethren—the *Unitas Fratrum*—who, in 1502, published a text called *Kinderfragen*. As early as 1518 Luther commenced to experiment with such books. His initial efforts were directed toward children, but in 1529 he published the *Large Catechism,* directly followed by the *Small Catechism,* as the basic texts of religious instruction for all ages. They were to be used assiduously in the family and by ministers and schoolmasters.

Luther declared, with characteristic recklessness, that those who refused to take the catechism seriously were to be told "that they deny Christ and are not Christians," and on that account were to be excluded from Holy Communion, refused baptism for their children, sent back to Rome, yea, to Satan himself.[8] His point was, as he himself once remarked,⁹ that the church only exists in vitality where God's people exercise themselves in God's Word—preach it, believe it, confess it, study it, and act it. Short of that there would come the inevitable relapse into trivial Christianity.

In Geneva, under Calvin's regime and in the Reformed churches at large, catechetical books were written for young and old; but no doubt they were employed especially to sustain family nurture. It was the rule in Geneva that parents must teach the catechism to their children at home and present them at church on Sunday, at noon, when they received additional instruction and were examined. Once a year the elders came round to each house to see if little Jacques knew what was the chief end of man. If his answer was other than God, the father of the household might well expect to be disciplined. When the child had learned the catechism to the satisfaction of the pastor, he recited the sum of it before the congregation as his profession of faith; and thereupon he was admitted for the first time to the Lord's Table.[10]

It is a very significant fact that the Reformers were intent upon making the Bible available in the vernacular to Everyman. It is also significant that they were committed to the cause of public education, without which man's access to the Scriptures would be severely limited, and his maturity in the Scriptures, almost impossible. Granted, then, that the Bible was now open to all Christians, why did the Reformers resort to the catechism? Luther customarily spoke of the catechism as "the right bible of the laity." Why was not "the right bible of the laity" the Bible itself? There are two broad answers to this question.

First, the Reformers were persuaded that the catechism was an indispensable aid to serious study of the Scriptures and to an enduring discipleship in God's Word. The grand design of catechetical books was to relate the believer more and more to scripture; and this they did in the following ways: (a) The catechism presented, in sum, the cardinal teachings of the holy Scriptures, which, as Calvin said, ought to be "common and familiar to all Christians."[11] For that reason also, Luther referred to such manuals as *Verbum Abbreviatum* (the Abbreviated Word).[12] (b) The catechism was intended to shed light on the Bible and on the preaching of the gospel in such fashion that simple folk would be led more and more to the apprehension of God's Word. But who were those "simple folk"? Read the preface to Luther's Large Catechism and you will see that the learned Reformer did not even exempt himself from that category. Neither Luther nor Calvin left the slightest doubt in their writings that they intended a lifelong discipleship to scripture, sermon, *and* catechism; and it is mistaken to believe that catechetics in the sixteenth century was merely a theology for children. In the Palatinate this principle is exactly illustrated by the requirement that ministers must preach regularly on questions of the Heidelberg Catechism, so that what one learned as a child was rehearsed and made ever more profound in the entire course of adult life. (c) Finally, the catechism related the believer to scripture by asking the question of scriptural relevance and meaning. *Was ist das?* is the key phrase of Luther's Catechism:

> I am the Lord thy God. Thou shalt have no other Gods before me.
> *Was ist das?* [What does this really mean in Christian life?]
> *Answer.* We should fear, love, and trust in God above all things.[13]

And this question of relevance was typical of almost all the great catechisms of the sixteenth century.

The second major explanation of the catechism lies in the fact that the Reformers were unwilling to suffer the objective character of the church or the consensus of Christian doctrine to be jeopardized by the subjective excursions of the believers into the Scriptures. "Observe well," said Calvin in a statement famous for its rejection of private opinion, "it is not said that God has left the Scriptures for everyone to read, but has appointed a government that there may be persons to teach."[14] The church, a government for Christian education! Indeed, to Calvin, the church is not only mother but teacher. "Such is our weakness," he added, "that we may not leave her school until we have spent the course of our lives as her pupils."[15] The catechism was one of the chief instruments of this corporate teaching function of the church. Surely it was no frivolous circumstance that in the *Kirchenrathsordnung* of 1564 all ministers and schoolmasters of the Palatinate

The Reformed Church in the Palatinate

were required to subscribe to the Heidelberg Catechism, and were solemnly enjoined to "apply it diligently to young and old," avoiding all "novelties" to the contrary.[16] So we are brought back to a Reformation principle which was enunciated earlier: Before the Word of God, the believer's responsibility was not one of private judgment, but one of serious discipleship.

THE REFORMED DOCTRINE OF THE MINISTRY

Our main concern here is to see in broad perspective how the Reformed churches conceived of the ministry. We must rely mainly on Calvin, taking care to note whatever correspondence exists between Calvin and the Palatinate standards. We must also confine ourselves to the pastor, leaving aside the other orders: teacher, elder, and deacon.

Calvin asserted, first of all, that the ministry is an "office" or "order" ordained by Jesus Christ.[17] The Palatinate *Kirchenrathsordnung* employed similar terms: either the German *Amt* (office) or the Latin *Vocatio* (a medieval term designating the monastic or priestly "call").[18] The nature of this "office" is given in the commission of Christ to his apostles: to preach the gospel, to baptize, and to deliver the Holy Communion. "Here," said Calvin, "is the holy, inviolable, and perpetual law imposed upon those who took the place of the apostles by which they received the command to preach the gospel and administer the sacraments."[19]

By the word office Calvin meant to deny that the ministry was merely an extension of the priesthood of all believers. "We must be careful," he warned, "not to confound the spiritual priesthood, common to all Christians, . . . with this outward and ministerial priesthood, which belongs, not to all, but to those alone who have been called and duly ordained to it."[20] Nor did Calvin countenance the idea that a minister simply performs a special *function* delegated to him out of the corporate ministry of the whole congregation. On the contrary, said he, "the government of the church by the ministry of the Word is not a contrivance of men, but an appointment made by the Son of God. . . . To Christ we owe it that we have ministers of the gospel, that they abound in necessary qualifications, and that they execute the trust committed to them. . . . All is his gift."[21]

It is, however, because Calvin took the Word of God so seriously that he took the ministry so seriously. For him, the Word and the ministry of the Word are inseparable gifts of God. In granting the church the written Word to be the source of its life, God has also furnished an order of ministers to publish and interpret the Word and to deliver it visibly in the sacraments, so that it is always real, alive, and effective in the experience of the church.[22] Here is the heart of what Calvin meant by the ministry. Borrowing from the apostle Paul, Calvin called it "the gift of interpretation."[23]

For Calvin, this "gift of interpretation" encompassed two profound services. First, it was the responsibility of the minister, and his alone, to break open the Word where it is hard, to divide it where it is unmanageable, to shed light upon it where it is obscure.[24] Scripture interpretation was not left open to Everyman. Throughout his commentaries, Calvin assailed two classes of men who despised the authority of the ministry: the spiritualist, whose private inspirations transcended the Scriptures, and the self-styled biblical expert who was all-knowing about scripture and instant to edify others. Wrote Calvin in his commentary on Ephesians:

> [There are] fanatics, on the one hand, who pretend to be favored with secret revelations of the Spirit, and proud men, on the other hand, who imagine that to them the private reading of the Scriptures is enough, and that they have no need of the . . . ministry of the church. . . . That those who neglect this instrument should hope to become perfect in Christ is utter madness.[25]

The other aspect of this "gift of interpretation" was even more impressive. With the other great Reformers, Calvin shared the view that true preaching is God speaking. The preached Word was a veritable means of grace by which God elected to address his people and to offer them his gifts of forgiveness, sonship, and a place within the family of faith. Therefore true preaching held the inevitable possibility that the ancient words of scripture and the human speech of the minister might, by the action of the Holy Spirit, spring alive in the hearts of the hearers and be heard

The Reformed Church in the Palatinate

as the real, alive, effective Word of God. Here, in Calvin's view, is the real *raison d'etre* of the ministry. On this account, he was willing to say that ministers are the Lord's ambassadors in the world, interpreters of his secret will, representatives of his person (*Institutes* 4:3:1). God's voice resounds in their speech; they speak "just as if he himself spoke" (*Institutes* 4:1:5). The ministry, Calvin concluded, is an "angelic office"; it literally replaces the ministry of angels, by whom Daniel was counseled (*Commentary on Daniel*, 7:15). For this very reason, "the Lord sent Philip to the eunuch rather than an angel . . . because he wanted to accustom us to hear men. This is assuredly no small commendation of external preaching that the voice of God soundeth in the mouth of men to our salvation, when angels hold their peace" (*Commentary on Acts*, 8:31).

With great candor, Calvin stated that men have not much choice about this. If they wish to hear God, they must hear his ministers. "God will not come down from heaven, neither will he send his angels to bring us revelations from above; but he will be made known to us by his Word; therefore he will have ministers of the church to preach his truth" (*Sermon on 1 Timothy*, 3:14). Calvin also warned that those who reject the ministry reject God. "Therefore, lest, like giants, we make war against God, let us learn to hearken to the ministers by whose mouth he teacheth us" (*Commentary on Acts*, 7:51). Finally, Calvin made it unmistakably clear that, by the design of Christ himself, the edification of the church proceeds from the ministry. "The church," he said, "is the common mother of all the godly, which bears, nourishes, and brings up children to God—kings and peasants alike; and this is done by the ministry. Those who neglect or despise this order choose to be wiser than Christ" (*Commentary on Ephesians*, 4:12). From this we see that "neither the light and heat of the sun, nor food and drink are so necessary to nourish and sustain the present life, as the apostolical and pastoral office is necessary to preserve the church on earth" (*Institutes* 4:3:2).

In keeping with this doctrine, Calvin insisted that the minister should not be heard as a private individual; his is a special, a public office.[26] This is the central significance of ordination, which means that the one ordained "is no longer a law unto himself, but bound in servitude to God and the church" and is commended as such to the people.[27] Similarly, the anointing of Isaiah meant that the prophet was no longer a private person, but henceforth discharged a public office.[28] By consequence, and without intending to impugn at all the ministry of the *laos,* Calvin denied that unordained persons should be allowed to preach or administer the sacraments. He wrote:

> No sound Christian makes all men equal in the administration of Word and sacraments, not simply on the pretext that all things ought to be done in the church decently and in order, but because, by the special command of Christ, ministers are ordained for that purpose.[29]

Zacharias Ursinus agreed: "The declaration of [God's] grace which is accomplished by the preaching of the gospel is committed to the ministers of Christ. The preaching of the gospel is committed to them alone."[30]

CHURCH LIFE IN THE PALATINATE

Faith, according to the Heidelberg Catechism, proceeds from the Holy Spirit, and is ordinarily wrought in our hearts by the preaching of the Word and the use of the sacraments (Question 65), both of which are delivered to the church by the office of the ministry. Life in the church thus commences with baptism. Ursinus did not treat this sacrament as clearly as he might have; and the problem is compounded by the fact that the English version of his Commentary[31] is not always faithful to the Latin. Nevertheless in at least four instances, Ursinus asserted that "in the legitimate use [of this sacrament] the delivery and reception of the signs and the delivery and reception of the things signified are joined."[32] Hence, baptism means that in and through this sacramental action *nos recipi a Deo in gratiam*[33] (God receives us into grace), God opens his arms to us and takes us into his favor. Ursinus did not mean that baptismal grace was a "thing" at all (it simply came out that way because he was bound to use the medieval term *res*). What he meant to say was that baptism was the action of being brought into a new relationship to God, the

The Reformed Church in the Palatinate

full character of which is recounted in Question 70 of the Catechism:

> It means to have the forgiveness of sins from God, through grace, for the sake of Christ's blood, . . . and to be renewed by the Holy Spirit and sanctified as members of Christ, so that we may more and more die unto sin and live in a consecrated and blameless way.

The new relationship also means specifically that we are translated from the world, "grafted into" the Christian church, introduced into a new sphere of grace and common life in the body of Christ.

Should infants be baptized—those who have not the robust commitment of the adult believer? The Catechism answers this question in the affirmative (Question 74). Children of Christian parents are born within the sphere of the church. They are accounted heirs of the covenant. Thus the gracious promises of the New Covenant, which are held out to these children of the church, should be established to them by baptism.[34] And thereby, as Calvin put it, "the seed of the faithful should be admitted into the fellowship of grace."[35] Reformed theology often supported that principle by other arguments, notably Calvin's idea of accommodation, reflections of which are also to be found in Ursinus. That is to say, the baptism of infants into the relationship of grace, is an "accommodation" to them by their kind heavenly Father—an accommodation which has its tokens in the very childhood of Jesus Christ and in Jesus' tender embraces of the little children who were brought to him. "How unjust of us," wrote Calvin, "to drive away those whom Christ calls to himself —to shut out those whom he willingly receives!"[36]

In the mystery of baptism, the child is not alone. In the way of all life, and especially of Christian life, he is supported by a community of faith, which speaks the baptismal vows corporately and faithfully on the child's behalf, and assumes the responsibility for his growth in the church, by virtue of which he may verify those vows in adult life. Thus, in the Palatinate, the baptism of infants was required to be given in the presence of the whole congregation, because (as the Liturgy so plainly said) the care and training of the child were committed to the *whole* community of faith, of which the parents and sponsors were surrogates, obliged to give the child Christian nurture on the church's behalf.[37]

The child was trained in the Catechism throughout his youth. When he was persuaded, by virtue of his personal faith and repentance, that he was ready to ratify his baptismal vow, he presented himself at the Preparatory Service, on the Saturday before Holy Communion. On that occasion he recited the Apostles' Creed, the Ten Commandments, and the Lord's Prayer, and certain parts of the Catechism as his profession of faith. That done, he was invited to join the congregation at the Lord's Table.[38] The connection implied here between baptism and the Lord's Supper is described by Ursinus. If baptism is the *sacramentum introitus* (the sacrament of entrance into the church), the Eucharist is the *sacramentum mansionis* (the sacrament of abiding in the church), in which, by faith, we receive the food and drink of eternal life, and become more and more united to the sacred Body of Jesus Christ.[39]

But the child's first communion did not bring to an end the usefulness of the Catechism. On the contrary, the Heidelberg Catechism was, above all, a book for adults, designed to direct and stimulate their lifelong discipleship to the Word of God. For that purpose, the Palatinate *Kirchenordnung* required catechetical preaching, a device probably brought over from the Lutheran churches in nearby Württemberg. Three provisions were made for the use of the Catechism in the context of public worship. At the principal service on Sunday morning, prior to the sermon, the minister was directed to read out several questions, following a given schedule which enabled him to cover the whole book in the course of nine weeks. Every Sunday afternoon a catechetical service was also held in a setting of worship. On that occasion the minister examined the children and proceeded to expound the Catechism to the whole congregation on a yearly cycle. Finally, the minister was encouraged to relate as many of his sermons to that manual as he could, whatever the occasion, taking care to inform his parishioners of the questions in the Catechism upon which his sermon had a bearing.[40]

From all this we can see that, in the Palatinate, catechetics was used to assist Christians to take the Word of God with seriousness. What one learned as a youthful catechumen became immeasurably more profound as life went on, through the faithful publication of the Heidelberg book.

At the very heart of this baptismal-catechetical religion was the Lord's Supper. It is well known that John Calvin ardently desired to celebrate the Eucharist every Sunday because of its exceeding profit. Yet despite his persistent efforts to achieve such an arrangement, he was overruled time and again by the Genevan magistrates who preferred the Zwinglian program of quarterly communion. The Palatinate Church was able to realize far more nearly Calvin's great desire. The *Kirchenordnung* of 1563 declared:[41]

> The Lord's Supper shall be observed at least once a month in the towns; once every two months in the villages; and on Easter, Pentecost, and Christmas in both places. Yet where the edification, custom, or need of the churches may necessitate, it is Christian and proper to observe it more often.

The great importance of this sacrament was expounded with considerable clarity in six questions of the Catechism (75-80) and in several collateral writings by Ursinus. The doctrine to be found in these texts was that of Calvin and Melanchthon. Calvin himself referred to it as the doctrine of the spiritual real presence. "Real" in this instance means that the sacrament is more than a spiritual refreshment, more than a memorial; it is even more than the "visible Word of God," unless you make it perfectly clear that that Word is the Savior himself, who is personally present to be received, trusted, and loved. The word real also specifies that the believer communicates not only with the Spirit of Christ, nor with his divine nature alone, but with Christ himself in his whole person, including his true and proper humanity, and hence with his very body and blood.

But this communion, while entirely real, is understood in a spiritual manner, as opposed to a local, corporal manner. According to Calvin and his colleagues, the essence of a living body does not consist of its chemical components, its material particles. The real identity of a body consists in its living energy, its animating power. Thus, to take the chemistry of Christ's body by mouth, even if that were literally possible, would be of little sustenance. What really happens in the Lord's Supper is that the living energy, the animating power of Christ's life—his vivific virtue, to use Calvin's terms—is brought over into the center of our lives, making us more and more one with Christ himself. "From the substance of his flesh," said Calvin, "Christ breathes life into our souls—indeed, pours forth his very life into us."[42] This animating power of Christ's life is, as Calvin said, nourishment for the soul. Thus it is received by faith, not by mouth. Nor is it fastened to the elements, as if it had dimensions; rather it is communicated through the sacramental mystery as a whole.

"Grace," said Melanchthon, "is not medicine, but good will."[43] Indeed, the Reformers were always intent upon saying that the grace of the Lord's Supper is not an infusion of subpersonal stuff, in the medieval sense, but God's personal love in action, bringing the sinner into fellowship with himself. In keeping with that conviction, the Heidelberg Catechism labored to make it clear —especially in Questions 76 and 79—that our reception of the grace of this sacrament, namely, the merits of Christ's suffering and death, is predicated upon a real life-union with Christ himself, powerfully wrought in our souls by the Holy Spirit. The strong reaction of the Reformation against the substance-theology of the Middle Ages, and the tendency of the Reformers to see the realities of Christianity in terms of persons and the relations of persons nevertheless created liturgical problems.

For both Calvin and Ursinus, the Lord's Supper was peculiarly the sacrament of the church. "This Holy Supper," said Calvin, was "ordained and instituted for joining the members of our Lord Jesus Christ with their head and one another in one body and one spirit."[44] Calvin meant that this sacrament "realized" the church as no other ecclesiastical action. That is precisely why he insisted the Supper be observed as often as the church assembled—at least every Sunday.[45] And that is also why the Reformed churches related discipline to the Lord's Supper, as the Heidelberg Catechism and the Palatinate Liturgy testify. For discipline served to guard the integrity of both the sacrament and the church against profanation by faithless and profligate persons who manifestly do not belong to Christ. Those who were "excommunicated" from Holy Communion—and there was a form for doing this in the Palatinate Liturgy itself—were by that very token cut off from the Christian communion itself, until they repented the error of their ways. Thus, as Questions 81-85 of the Catechism declare, the critical issue of the whole Christian life was fitness to approach the Lord's Table.

Calvin[46] and Ursinus[47] were generally agreed that discipline accomplishes three purposes: First, it enables the church to be itself—to be vital, authentic, unspoiled by hypocrisy. Discipline restrains, stimulates, chastens, promotes order and unity; enforces doctrine and makes it effective in human life. Thus Calvin could say, "As the saving doctrine of Christ is the soul of the church, so discipline forms the ligaments which then connect the members together."[48] Second, the correction of discipline prompts men to repent. Third, discipline is a principle of restraint, a principle of moral example which is likely to have a beneficial effect upon society at large.

Behind all of this stands ultimately the great Calvinistic virtue of obedience to the will of God. If Luther dwelt upon the consolations of grace, Calvin could not forget the implicit demands of grace. For him, election means that the entire Christian life is to be devoted to the glory of God; and God's glory attains its highest human expression in man's obedience and sanctity. The third part of the Heidelberg Catechism participates in this spirit, in this austere heroism and deliberate obedience that shaped the Calvinist piety.

THE REFORMED DOCTRINE OF THE CHURCH

So the true shape of Palatinate religion begins to emerge. Christianity, as the theologians of Frederick the Pious conceived it, rested in the corporate experience of the church; for they understood the church to be the bearer of spiritual life to her children. We have seen a vigorous parochial life, established upon baptism, edified by a lifelong use of the Catechism, nourished by the Lord's Supper, protected and invigorated by discipline. In short we have encountered substantial churchmanship; one might even say, high churchmanship.

Yet there appears to be a profound contradiction between this conception of the church and the doctrine of election which is represented in certain questions of the Heidelberg Catechism and implied in others. For if my salvation resides entirely in the eternal decrees of God, how can the visible institutions of the church make any conceivable difference? This problem becomes especially acute if you define the true church, as Calvin did in the first edition (1536) of the *Institutes,* as the whole company of the elect, known only to God, and therefore invisible.[49]

Even so, Calvin had to confront the practical and unavoidable question: Is there any way by which I may be assured of election, by which I may really experience my participation in the church? Such assurance, said Calvin, does not come to us by some extraordinary perception into the hidden decrees of God, as if we were able to spy our name in the heavenly register. A frivolous notion! But it does assuredly come by what Calvin designates "our inward calling," namely, our conscious awareness that the Word of God *has* come alive in our hearts through the action of the Holy Spirit and that we *do* indeed belong to Christ through faith.[50]

Here is the sign of our election. And here is the only certification of church membership which has any profound worth, for it depends upon our believing fellowship with Christ. According to this spirit, the Heidelberg Catechism presented the doctrine of election, not as a conundrum to try the intellect, but rather, as our only comfort in life and in death (Question 1), the stimulus of our moral life (Question 32), and the basis of our undoubted membership in the church (Question 54).

Yet there is, in fact, another dimension to Calvin's theology; and its architectonic principle is high churchmanship. The visible structures of the church—the ministry of Word and sacraments, catechetical instruction, parochial discipline—these remain as the means of grace. For these are the very ways which God himself appointed to declare and seal to us the promises of the gospel. These are the channels through which the external decree of God's grace is conveyed in historic time. As J. S. Whale observes,[51] Christ the Redeemer is the supreme means of grace. "As prophet, priest, and king, the Incarnate Son is the actualization in time of

The Reformed Church in the Palatinate

the eternal Father's will to save us. The church is, as it were, his outward and visible body; it is not only relevant but indispensable." Therefore, the church is both invisible but undeniably, indispensably visible.

In the later editions of the *Institutes,* this side of Calvin's thought, this emphasis upon the church in its empirical actuality, became the predominate concern of his ecclesiology. And in the *Institutes* of 1559 he was prepared to say—in words which were astonishingly like those of Cyprian—that we should not entertain any ordinary prospects of salvation apart from Christian nurture in the visible church.[52] According to this shift in his thought, Calvin tended more and more to say that our election is to be defined and recognized by our participation in the life of that visible church.

Thus in the final analysis, election produces, not an atomistic individualism as we might logically suppose, but an empirical church of believers, chosen by God for himself, where his Word is truly preached and heard, where the sacraments are administered according to Christ's institution, where discipline stimulates the community and guards its integrity, where worship is understood to mean the liturgy of the elect who gather to hear God's most holy Word and to set forth his most worthy praise—where, in sum, God has *deposited* the treasures of his grace.[53] Hence Calvinism makes provision for churchmanship; and that characteristic is readily detected in the church life of the Palatinate.

THE PALATINATE LITURGY

Viewed from our own situation in the last two hundred years, the Palatinate Liturgy[54] has something to commend it. It was a *liturgy*. It was a liturgy which took doctrine very seriously. It was a liturgy which managed to relate the Word in sermon and sacrament far more acceptably than many churches today, involving, as it did, the celebration of Holy Communion at least once a month.

If there are certain exaggerations in this liturgy—a certain barrenness, a certain didactic tyranny, a certain disregard for the classic shape of the Western rite—these occurred, no doubt, because of the frank opposition by Reformed churchmen to the errors of Rome. The opposition, of which I speak, took three particular forms.

First, in contrast to the Roman idea that tradition constituted a source of authority independent of scripture, Calvin insisted that the Word alone can prescribe for the church. He applied that principle of authority also to the liturgy. To the ways of worship set forth in scripture, said Calvin, the church must adhere "with the least possible admixture of human invention."[55]

Second, alongside this positive principle of scriptural authority went another policy which shaped Reformed worship and which might be called "the seriousness of symbolism." Here the Calvinists found themselves at odds, not merely with the Romans, but with the Lutherans and Anglicans as well; for they took the position that if one meant to give the New Testament gospel a clear and authentic expression in the life of the church, then one could not afford to patch up the medieval symbols and expect them to suffice. Luther, who feared radical innovations, tried to purify and thereby retain as much of the old cultus as he could. Even the Elevation managed to survive in his Evangelical Mass as a kind of pictorial sermon. To Calvin, that policy was unthinkable —a sure guarantee of ambiguity and confusion. The Reformed churches were determined to abolish those symbols which were apt to be misleading, ambiguous, or merely vapid. Only those forms were kept or added which expressed the gospel with real clarity and power. Thus the mood of the Reformed churches everywhere tended to be one of austerity, authenticity, clarity, and forcefulness. But, alas, the luxuriant growth of medieval ceremonies was too often replaced by a grossness of words, which made everything rather too plain, too didactic, depriving the liturgy of its proper sense of action and mystery.

Third, the Reformed theologians were concerned to correct the medieval conception of grace as a quasi-material stuff, a divine vitamin infused in man's soul through the sacraments. When they spoke of justification by grace through faith, they meant grace in the biblical, evangelical sense of forgiveness and reconciliation. God opens his arms to me. I am judged sinner and taken as son. What was subpersonal has become personal. Similarly in the Lord's Supper, grace involves the personal communion with Christ. But then, shall we consecrate the Eucharistic elements? Shall we revert to the medieval idea and assume that grace does have dimensions after all? That was the quandary. And Calvin never solved it. The Reformed rites tried to consecrate people rather than elements, on the supposition, no doubt, that the people were the ones to be prepared for this personal encounter with Christ.

When we turn to the Palatinate Liturgy itself, we discover at once that the Ante-Communion does not follow the Genevan model exactly, but involves certain structural deficiencies. Even so it participates deeply in the Reformed liturgical spirit with all its massive soberness, and contains the classic Reformed features, some of which deserve our attention. The Liturgy commences with the solemn Prayer of Confession from the Genevan rite. In "well-ordered churches" wrote Calvin, confession is the proper beginning of worship; for it brings men to "a true estimation" of themselves; and by the very acknowledgment of their wretchedness, they also acknowledge "the goodness and mercy of our God." And thus, as Calvin put it, "the gate of prayer is opened."[56] He insisted, moreover, that confession deserved to be followed by absolution. When the people have thrown themselves on God's mercy, he wrote, "it is no mean or trivial consolation to have Christ's ambassador present, furnished with the mandate of reconciliation."[57] In this respect also, the Palatinate Liturgy adhered to Calvin's ideas. In fact, it succeeded where Calvin failed, for the magistrates of Geneva refused to countenance an absolution.

But for some reason, Olevianus and his colleagues saw fit to include two confessions. The second one, which directly followed the sermon, was typically Lutheran, cast in the first person singular and drawn verbatim from the Württemberg Liturgy.[58] Under these circumstances, the Absolution was necessarily displaced. It was nevertheless a forthright declaration of the gospel promises, cast in words which still live among us: "Hearken now to the undoubted comfort of the grace of God which he doth promise in his gospel to all that believe."[59]

In the Calvinist rites generally, proclamation was the next major feature of the liturgy. It consisted of three parts which were never to be separated: a collect for illumination by the Holy Spirit[60]; the lesson read out of scripture; the sermon. In this arrangement we see the very heart of the Reformed doctrine of preaching. Here are Spirit, Word, ministry inseparably associated in this marvelous communication. For his part, the minister must bind himself to scripture, treating it with the utmost reverence and humility. Such, said Calvin, is his "spiritual chastity."[61] At the same time, if the prayers of the church are answered, the Holy Spirit illuminates and quickens the Word, so that it springs alive in the congregation, and becomes in fact God's Word—God speaking. As Calvin put it: "The voice which is in itself mortal, is made an instrument to communicate eternal life."[62]

The Communion Liturgy was designed to be inserted into the Sunday service immediately prior to the closing psalm. At his station "by the table," the minister delivered the long Exhortation that was typical of the Calvinist rite. It opened with the Words of Institution (1 Corinthians 11), which served two basic functions, corresponding to the two principal parts of the Exhortation.

First, in keeping with Paul's warning against unworthy participation, the people were admonished earnestly to search their hearts; and those were invited to the Table who sought their life in Christ, knowing that they lived in the midst of death. But those, on the contrary, whose faithfulness or obduracy disqualified them as true disciples were fenced from that table, not by name, but rather by a recital of their crimes: "All adulterers, fornicators, drunkards, thieves, usurers, robbers, gamblers, misers" and so on and on. While this emphasis upon introspection and exclusion spoiled the Eucharistic spirit and the social character of the Supper, Calvin's usage, as usual, had some purpose to it. To him, as we have explained before, the integrity of both sacrament and church was at stake. If just anyone were invited to the Lord's Table, seemingly without jeopardy to himself or without profanation of the mystery, would not the objective potency of the sacrament and the reality of its grace be called into serious question? And if the Supper were merely a random gathering of sundry decent folk, where was the church to be truly seen, and what sense was left to this ancient "Liturgy of the Faithful"? These were Calvin's thoughts, which he commenced to express as early as 1537.

Second, the Words of Institution included the *command* of Christ, to which the sacrament owes its origin, and the *promises* of Christ, in the sure hope of which the church observes the sacrament. In the second part of the Reformed Communion Exhortation, those promises were rehearsed in considerable detail. They were literally "preached," to use Calvin's term. Why? The answer is laid out in Book IV of the *Institutes,* beginning at chapter 14. Here Calvin developed a theology of consecration. The Word, he said, must be added to the sacrament for the sake of its efficacy. Specifically the divine promises annexed to the sacrament—the promises of Christ which underlie the Supper—must be applied in order to give meaning and reality to the signs. But exactly what is to be consecrated? The answer is clearly: the people. The consecrating Word is addressed to them. They, as persons, must be prepared for the personal grace of the sacrament. This, said Calvin, is the prime error of Roman priests who neglect the Word but attempt rather to effect the consecration of *elements* "by murmuring and gesticulating in the manner of sorcerers." Their means and their end are both wrong. What is required to season this sacramental action is not an "incantation" over the bread and wine, but "the lively preaching of the promises of Christ," addressed to the congregation.[63]

The problem of the Eucharistic elements is further complicated by the fact that the Reformed theologians, in faithfulness to the language of scripture, placed the risen body of Christ at the right hand of the Father in heaven. By consequence they taught that this "vast interval of space," which separates Christ and the earthly pilgrim, is overcome by the "miraculous" action of the Holy Spirit who raises the believer to the presence of the Savior on high. According to this teaching, the role of the communion elements was thrown into greater confusion. To illustrate this new problem, let me quote first from the Genevan Catechism[64]:

> *Question.* Then you think that the body is not enclosed within the bread?

Answer. By no means. Rather I think that in order to enjoy the reality of the signs, our minds must be raised to heaven where Christ is. . . . But in these earthly elements it is improper and vain to seek him.

And now compare the final exhortation in the Palatinate Liturgy, which appeared in virtually all of the Reformed rites immediately before the distribution of the elements:

> That we may now be fed with Christ, . . . let us not cleave . . . to this external bread and wine, but lift up our hearts and our faith into heaven, where Jesus Christ is our Intercessor at the right hand of his heavenly Father.[65]

Thus these earthly signs—plain bread and wine—these signs of God's "coming down" to us, were wrenched of their true meaning, and fairly obliterated themselves as they became vehicles to transport us above all things earthly and visible to the far reaches of heaven.

So, we have been confronted by one of the major problems of Reformed Eucharistic theology and of Reformed liturgics: What is to be said and done about the elements? John Nevin stated the matter bluntly: "The Reformed doctrine admits no change whatever in the elements. Bread remains bread, and wine remains wine."[66] Calvin, at least, left the matter in considerable confusion. In *Institutes* 4:17:14 he approved the type of consecration used by the ancient fathers: "They say that in consecration a secret conversion takes place so that there is now something other than bread and wine." By that they meant that the elements "have to be considered a different class from common foods . . . since in them is set forth the spiritual food and drink of the soul. This we do not deny." Yet Calvin's liturgy was notoriously devoid of just this sort of consecration. And in his treatise *Reforming the Church,* he said with flat defiance: "The whole force of the consecration is directed to us, not to the bread and wine."[67]

Calvin's treatment is unsatisfactory. It is a dubious idea that a liturgy "preaches." It is equally dubious that good sacramental theology will allow us to leave the signs in the uncertain state that Calvin does. The solution is hardly simple, considering the many facets of the problem which have been noted. The issue is

The Reformed Church in the Palatinate

especially important in the light of contemporary theology, which is newly concerned to stress the *personal* character of grace in view of the depersonalization of man in modern culture. Throughout his writings, Calvin speaks of the mystical sacramental union which subsists between the realities and the signs. He used that term to distinguish his own position from the Roman tendency to identify symbol and reality and the Zwinglian tendency to divorce them. Part of the answer to this problem may lie in a careful reading of Calvin to determine exactly what he means by that "mystical, sacramental union."[68]

CONCLUSION

In part I have tried here to act as historian, and to improve upon certain misunderstandings which have arisen of late about the Reformed heritage.

In part, also, I have tried to assess the relevance of the old Palatinate religion for our own time. The forms of that religion are probably not nearly so significant as the ideas they evoke. In the Catechism, for example, we see more than questions and answers; we see a deep concern on the part of our predecessors to relate the believer profoundly to the Word of God. We see the idea of a discipleship to the Word, which gives religion depth, and empowers the mutual priesthood of all believers. Even more important, we see in the Catechism a middle way between the dictated faith of the medieval church, and, at the other extreme, the vast subjectivism which infects the modern church.

From the Reformed doctrine of the ministry we learn chiefly that if we propose to take the Word of God seriously, we must take the ministerial office seriously, as these are the inseparable gifts of God to his church. The delivery of that Word in sermon and sacrament, involving, as it does, the possibility of God speaking and thus of faith and eternal life, cannot be assigned to Everyman, whatever his spiritual competence may be. The edification of the church, being a matter of the most solemn gravity, is entrusted to an order of ministers, commissioned by Christ himself. J. S. Whale defends the Reformed doctrine correctly when he says, "Calvin restores authority to the ministry because, and only because, it is nothing less than the ministry *of the Word of God.*"⁶⁹ To this it is fair to add that Calvin was apt to stress the responsibilities and perils of the ministry, rather than its prerogatives.

In the same connection, the Palatinate standards encourage us —now that the liturgical revival is in actual progress—to devote our concern also to a renewal of preaching, along Reformation lines, and to the reinstatement of the Calvinist doctrine of the Supper, which is not everywhere confirmed among us, and to the recovery of the ancient union of Word and sacrament, or at least a more proportionate balance between them.

The Palatinate Liturgy, for all its faults, will not let us forget that symbolism, in all forms, is a critical matter, with the potential of either conveying or confounding the gospel. One thinks of a church where the little red lights of the Holy Spirit are "rheostated" off when the sermon begins. The old Palatinate order teaches us that true liturgy exists in the most intimate bond with doctrine. Some of our brothers, lately assembled in Rome, put it in this fashion:

> Liturgy is in some way
> dogma lived in the most sacred moments:
> the Bible prayed;
> the spirituality of the church in its most characteristic act;
> the culmination and source of all her activity.⁷⁰

CHAPTER THREE

The Catechism and the Mercersburg Theology

IN 1827, at the Synod of York, Pastor John Smaltz surveyed the state of the German Reformed Church:

> God "has not utterly forsaken us," he said, "yet the state of religion in our bounds is . . . extremely low. There is much ignorance and irreligion with which we have to contend, and an awful deadness in spiritual matters. . . . Perhaps no religious community in our country needs the special mercies of heaven . . . more than ours."[1]

Part of the problem lay in the simple statistics which he quoted: 30,000 communicants, 400 congregations, 90 pastors. Because of the great lack of ministers, many outlying charges scarcely knew the benefit of a sustained parochial life. The younger clergy were trained irregularly in the parlors of their elders. This grievous problem the Synod now resolved to meet by a theological seminary, newly opened at Carlisle, established mainly on good intentions.

The invasion of the English language, moreover, had become an occasion of great scandal in this German Zion, splitting its urban congregations, exposing its tender flocks to all the vagaries of American religion.

The Reformed folk, being somewhat uncertain at this time of their separate mission, were closely drawn to their Lutheran brethren, with whom they shared the German heritage, as well as Pennsylvania farmland, union churches, and Luther's Bible. Between them they negotiated in the 1820's and 1830's toward a single "evangelical" church, based on a deliberate reduction of doctrine, which in fact had already occurred on both sides. But it came to naught.[2]

THE NEW MEASURES

At least the "awful deadness" which Smaltz lamented was soon to be dispelled. In 1828 the German Reformed Church entered upon a new era of revivals—an era which brought a certain recovery of spirit, plus all the entanglements that go with such manifestations. The less urbane revivalist was apt to employ mechanical effects and to generate intense excitement, with the object of assisting the sinner to "get religion." These radical techniques were called the "New Measures" or sometimes "Finneyism" after Charles G. Finney, the celebrated revival preacher, who depreciated the stated means of grace and designed his protracted meetings to elicit the sinner's "instant surrender to God." One of Finney's accessories was the "Anxious Bench."[3]

The revival spirit swept into both of the German churches. Benjamin Kurtz, editor of the influential *Lutheran Observer*, ventured to endorse the New Measures and thus made them attractive to his constituents. In the Reformed Church there was stiffer resistance to extravagance; but it was perfectly acceptable to believe in "true revivals"—a concept, however, which turned out to be rather elusive. Already the Reformed Church had suffered two secessions over the broad issue of revivalism: that of the United Brethren, around the turn of the century; and later that of John Winebrenner, pastor at Harrisburg, who founded the Churches of God.

In 1828 Finney launched a campaign in Philadelphia.[4] Presently Samuel Helffenstein, who was the soul of Reformed propriety, invited him to use the Race Street Church, largest in the city. There Finney conducted his "anxious meetings" which *The Magazine of the German Reformed Church* reported as follows:

> Sinners "were urged to immediate repentance and faith, and warned of the awful consequences of procrastination. . . . Arrows of conviction were hurled at the hearts of sinners, and instances of conversion occurred at almost every meeting."[5]

From that starting point until the middle 1840's, revivals were held in all quarters of the church. They in turn brought into vogue prayer meetings, sabbath schools, tract societies, temperance campaigns, sabbath observance, and missionary enterprises.

The Catechism and the Mercersburg Theology

The Messenger of the German Reformed Church did not fail to announce in its columns each new outbreak of these "refreshments"; and the Classes duly noted them in their reports to the Synod. In 1841 the Classis of Maryland was pleased to note "copious refreshings from the presence of the Lord," and added: "The dead, dry bones have been resuscitated from the death of sin and clothed with living beauty. They have become an army of saints in the camp of Israel's God and many of them are now actively engaged in winning, warming, encouraging, and directing sinners to the Savior."[6]

By that time, however, there was evidently some need to restrain this enthusiasm, lest it fall into Finneyism. The Synod struggled to find some medium, some new principle, between rationalistic formalism, on the one hand, and New Measures "fanaticism" on the other—or as young Pastor John Bomberger put it: between "no-fire" and "wild-fire."[7]

By and large, then, the German Reformed Church shared the inordinate anxiety of the Evangelical Revival to bring all men to the crisis of conversion. In 1840 Jacob Helffenstein preached at the Seminary (by then at Mercersburg) on the "Nature and Reality of Revivals." "A church without a revival," he said, "is in a guilty state and should be abased on account of her declension and apathy." God's work in conversion "is effected by human agency." If young preachers "do not become wise to win souls, all their other wisdom will avail them nothing."[8]

Helffenstein was simply reiterating the current doctrine that countless of the unconverted languished in every congregation, and that it was the church's business to reach these people by every available means; especially by those marvelous instruments: the sermon and free prayer. Beneath that idea lay a deeper one, namely, that there were two main points around which the Christian religion revolved: first, conversion, whereby one properly entered the church; second, zeal in moralistic and evangelistic enterprises—temperance societies, prayer meetings, and such—as evidence of sanctification. By consequence, the church was defined as an aggregation of the converted who were held together by external means. At the Synod of 1841 Bernard C. Wolff preached on "the true idea of the church" which he understood to be simply "a body of believers organized under the same government," doctrines, worship, and duties.[9]

THE CATECHISM AND THE LITURGY

How did the Heidelberg Catechism fare in this period? At first it was left to compete with at least eight private catechisms, some of which made no pretense of being in the Heidelberg tradition at all. But the Constitution of 1828 endorsed only the Heidelberg formulary and required the theological professors to use it authoritatively in their teaching. In the Mayer Liturgy subscription to the Catechism was required at ordination. And these and other safeguards were written into the Constitution of 1846. But whether the Heidelberg Catechism lived at the center of church life is another question entirely. It did not, at least, command attention in the columns of *The Messenger,* or in the deliberations of the Synod. Catechetical instruction, in any case, was a rather poor conductor of revival electricity. The *Lutheran Observer* knew a pastor who, at morning worship, received his catechumens into full communion, and that night invited them to the Mourner's Bench to get religion.[10]

The Palatinate Liturgy was consigned to much greater obscurity. The patriarchs had used a variety of German liturgies, brought over from abroad, and no doubt the Palatinate book had enjoyed greater use than the rest. But the change in language, which was well under way by 1820, meant that the church could no longer count on German to preserve its liturgical customs, but must face the full impact of American free worship.

Two books of services were published in the eastern segment of the church: the Germantown Liturgy (1798) and the Mayer Liturgy (1841). Neither made provision for the service of the Lord's Day; for even in the German Reformed Church it had become the rubric that Sunday worship must be free. But like all free services, the one normally used in Reformed congregations had a distinct form—and it happened to be the form of the Westminster *Directory,* quintessence of Puritan worship. It consisted of a sermon or lecture, with a long prayer before, and a short prayer after, and a hymn here and there to garnish the whole. All the prayers were free except the Lord's Prayer which

The Catechism and the Mercersburg Theology

was said by the minister. The Confession of Sin was consigned to the Preparatory Service. At Holy Communion, which was held twice yearly, the people were allowed to follow after the minister as he recited the Creed, provided they did so "in a low voice."[11] *The Messenger* complained that in some quarters even congregational singing had become obsolete. Of the church year, Good Friday itself was no longer kept.[12]

The premium on freedom rested in two considerations: first, the Puritan idea that "stinted" forms could not express the momentary needs of a given congregation, but succeeded only in stifling the real inspiration to prayer, stirred by the Holy Spirit; second, the needs of the revivalist, whose prayers as well as his sermons were implements of conversion, and who could not be bothered in the midst of a revival by a book full of forms.

The Synod made one attempt to bring out a book of worship; but the so-called Mayer Liturgy[13] had none of the virtues of a liturgy and it failed. What then? No translation of the Palatinate Liturgy had ever been made. And the German text, having been superseded in Germany, became so rare in this country that when a copy turned up at Easton in the 1840's, it caused a sensation.

The columns of *The Messenger* and the speakers at Synod left no doubt that Zwingli was the founder of the German Reformed Church. How could that be? Was Ursinus a Zwinglian after all? And the Heidelberg Catechism, a Zwinglian text? Such questions were never discussed; but the evidence does indicate that this congeniality on the part of the church toward the Swiss Reformer resided precisely in his doctrine of the Lord's Supper. In 1841 a correspondent to *The Messenger* who signed himself "A Zwinglian" offered the readers of that magazine "the rational, scriptural, and generally admired and adopted view of the pious and immortal Zwingli, concerning the Lord's Supper."[14] The connection drawn by that correspondent (and he was by no means the only one[15]) became explicit in the uncomplicated memorialism of the Mayer Liturgy. Here we are told that "an absent friend is easily forgotten" (the absent friend being Jesus); hence the purpose of this "ordinance" (Mayer did not like the word sacrament) is to help us to remember Christ's passion and to "feel near to God."[16]

DENOMINATIONAL SPIRIT

Around 1840 a rebirth of denominational spirit came over the church. That year Samuel Helffenstein advised the Synod of Greencastle (Pennsylvania) that there were now within its confines 75,000 souls, 600 congregations, and 184 ministers.[17] Among other favorable signs, he noted that the Seminary at Mercersburg had become the grand ornament of the church and guaranteed her ministry. At the next Synod, Bernard C. Wolff ventured to interpret these statistics. In the bygone days of our weakness, he said, we were tempted to unite with one of the more powerful churches. No more. "The time for . . . union with any other denomination has forever passed away." The one thing necessary now is to regain our self-consciousness as a denomination and exalt "all that distinguishes it from" others. The Reformed Church, he concluded, is perfect in every part: "It wants no further Reformation."[18]

This new sentiment was eagerly taken up by all manner of speakers and writers. Cried Bomberger: "May we love our Zion more and more. . . . Her peculiarities are not our own to throw away."[19] Meanwhile a scheme came out of the Maryland Classis to celebrate the centenary of the German Reformed Church. A circular was prepared in 1840, which, having paid its respects to "Zwinglius . . . that great Reformer of blessed memory," proceeded to set the tone of the celebration:

> Let the Centenary be an occasion for rallying around the standards of the church. . . . Let the idea be forever silenced that the interests of religion require the German Reformed Church to merge itself in other denominations or lay aside its distinctive character.[20]

With the revival of denominational spirit came a new view of Reformed history. It was outlined in a spate of sermons and articles[21] of the early 1840's in approximately this form: Polycarp, disciple of John and Bishop of Smyrna, founded a mission at Lugdunum in Gaul. In the persecutions of A.D. 177, refugees from that church fled into the Alps, where in the sixteenth century their descendants established the Reformed Church. But other commentators said this was wrong: the descendants of the refugees reappeared first in the twelfth century as followers of Peter

Waldo, and thus the Reformed Church was really neo-Waldensian.

This curious history served two purposes. Wolff used it to suggest that Lutheranism, by comparison, was a mere novelty. "We Reformed," he said, "are older stock."[22] Joseph Berg[23] employed it in a profounder way, namely, to support the idea of a perfect and changeless orthodoxy, which, being entirely untainted by Romanism, traces back through the Waldensians to apostolic times.

Connected with this view was a virulent anti-Catholicism which colored Protestant opinion generally in the 1840's. John Nevin, the new professor at Mercersburg, reviewed Berg's *Lectures on Romanism* and declared that the little book was sufficient "to drag some of the most hideous features of the Romish system into the broad light of day."[24] In 1842 *The Messenger* carried four articles on the question: "Does the Roman Catholic Church constitute any part of the church of Christ?"[25] The point is that the last thing a typical American Protestant wanted to believe in 1840 was that the Reformation had connections with medieval Catholicism. The only idea which could have been more perplexing was the idea of an evangelical Catholicism.

JOHN W. NEVIN

John Williamson Nevin and Philip Schaff came to Mercersburg at a time of high opportunity. They were swept into prominence by a ground swell of denominational spirit. Nevin, who preceded Schaff by four years, was inaugurated in May of 1840. The little Scotch-Irishman, who had lately taken up German to read Neander and was now enamored of German scholarship, sounded fairly Teutonic in his inaugural address, in which he appealed vastly to the new confessionalism:

> The German Church must rise within herself. . . . She must adhere to her own standards. She must have her own ministry. . . . She should continue to cherish still her national sympathies and hallowed associations for her own faith and worship.[26]

Nevin declared that the basis of his teaching would be the Old School Calvinist orthodoxy, to which he had been accustomed, now reestablished upon the Heidelberg Catechism. He remained in all respects a conservative evangelical, nicely turned out by Princeton Seminary. He was admittedly antiliturgical. He drew his most scandalous illustrations from the black record of the medieval church.[27] He was conspicuous for his promotions of moralistic causes. His only irregularity was a firm subscription to Calvin's doctrine of the Lord's Supper.[28] With respect to revivals Nevin scarcely knew his own mind. He assailed the "spiritual quackery" of the New Measures. But let anyone attack experimental religion and he was instant to defend it. Did not the Catechism teach "heart religion from beginning to end"?[29]

Yet Nevin suspected that the platform of Calvinist orthodoxy had become rickety in the German Church and he proposed to shore it up. From his hand came twenty-nine articles on the Heidelberg Catechism which graced *The Messenger* through most of 1840-1842. They read nicely until installment seven,[30] when Nevin ventured the opinion that Zwingli's Eucharistic doctrine was "low" and "rationalistic," for which reason the Reformed churches soon rejected it. That brought letters to the editor. In the eighteenth installment, Nevin reported Calvin's sacramental views in the following manner: "In the Lord's Supper, an actual union is realized on the part of the believer with the life of the Savior's glorified body."[31] And that, he added with obvious satisfaction, is the doctrine taught by the Heidelberg Catechism.

THE ANXIOUS BENCH AND CATHOLIC UNITY

To stimulate parochial life and curb fanaticism, Nevin was intent upon an established ministry in every charge. He prodded the congregation in Mercersburg to set the example. Thus at the close of 1842, the local Reformed folk heard a trial sermon by William Ramsey, whom Nevin had known at Princeton. On Sunday night, at the close of an emotional service, Ramsey issued an altar call to the packed audience, whereupon two elderly ladies started forward and the full excitement of the New Measures broke out. When the tumult abated, Nevin told the congregation in a few parting words that while they had got some fairly good exercise they should not assume to have progressed in piety.

The upshot was that Ramsey was grievously offended and declined the call, bringing on a crisis in the congregation, which

The Catechism and the Mercersburg Theology

spread into the Seminary, where not a few of the students were addicted to the New Measures. Nevin resolved to disinfect Mercersburg of this contagion by publishing, in the fall of 1843, a decisive little tract called *The Anxious Bench*.

The purpose of the tract was to disentangle Finneyism from the general cause of revivals in which Nevin earnestly believed. He declared that he had no hostility toward "meetings for prayer, protracted meetings, . . . pungent, earnest appeals to the conscience," and the like. Rather, his ire was directed against the "particular system of religious action" represented by the Anxious Bench. That system, he said, is "quackery"—one vast business of excitement which assaults man's nervous system and appeals to his fear and sympathy. It stands for justification by feeling—conversion willy-nilly, without faith or sanctification. Its practitioners are "wonder-workers" without any authenticity as ministers, without knowledge, personal holiness, or patience to press the claims of the gospel soberly. As churches it produces hodgepodges of people who have no common life, except it be mere sectarianism.

True revivals, Nevin contended, spring from another system altogether, namely, the system of the catechism, which includes sound preaching, faithful instruction, pastoral visitation, discipline. "Where these are fully employed," he counseled, "there will be revivals." Thus for Nevin a true revival was one which welled up out of parochial life and had its ballast in Bible and catechism, sound preaching and discipline, rather than some manipulated spectacle imposed on the congregation from without.

THE MERCERSBURG DOCTRINE OF THE CHURCH

The tract caused a sensation. After a stunned silence, the venerable fathers of the church pronounced in favor of Nevin. Even Henry Harbaugh, a student at the Seminary, hazarded the opinion that Nevin was right. The first edition of the tract was soon exhausted; and in 1844 Nevin brought out a second, in which the sixth chapter was rewritten and a seventh chapter appended.[32] Here he expounded for the first time the Mercersburg doctrine of the church. Later the same year Nevin amplified that doctrine in his sermon "Catholic Unity."[33]

According to the New Measures, Nevin observed, conversion

was presumed to be the product of the sinner's own will. That presumption struck him as a completely false analysis of both man's predicament and man's recovery. "Sin," he said, "is not simply the offspring of a particular will . . . but a wrong habit of humanity itself. . . . The disease is organic, rooted in the race" of Adam; and it cannot be overcome "by a force less deep and general than itself." Thus, he continued, "humanity, fallen in Adam, is made to undergo a resurrection in Christ," who is not merely a man, but *the* man, the second Adam, comprehending in his person the new creation—humanity recovered and redeemed.[34] Already the doctrine of the Second Adam and the New Creation had come to the forefront of Nevin's thought; already the incarnation tended to govern his thinking about redemption and the church.

How then does the sinner attain solidarity with this New Humanity? He does so, according to Nevin, "by an inward, living union with Christ" that is "as real as the bond by which he was joined in the first instance to Adam." Nevin left no doubt about the reality of the so-called Mystical Union—a conception which he repeatedly assigned to Calvin. At regeneration, he said, the Christian "is inwardly united to Christ by the power of the Holy Spirit. . . . A divine seed is implanted in him, the germ of a new existence, which is destined gradually to grow and gather strength, till the whole man shall be at last fully transformed into its image."[35] In the mystery of Holy Communion, Nevin saw the very epitome of this union which subsists between the believer and the person of Christ.

The church, as he now conceived it, is the historical continuation of the life of Jesus Christ in the world, and the only medium of his saving presence among men. Just as Adam lives in the human race generically, and *through* the race in every individual, so "Christ lives in the church, and *through* the church in its particular members."[36] Thus, if a man is saved at all, he is saved by the force of a spiritual constitution, namely the church, established by God to bear the life of Christ to fallen humanity through its ministry and sacraments. To Nevin it had become unthinkable to discuss the church as an aggregation of believers brought together by external means into a pious sodality. The

The Catechism and the Mercersburg Theology

church, he said emphatically, "is truly the mother of all her children. They do not impart life to her, but she imparts life to them."[37]

In his sermon on catholic unity, Nevin gave new importance to the visible church. He dispensed, in fact, with the old visible-invisible distinction and introduced a new set of categories: the ideal and actual church. The key to Nevin's meaning lay in the word potentially. In potency, the church includes within itself from the first all that it can ever become. In this sense it is ideal. By virtue of the same potency, however, the ideal church struggles constantly to become itself, yet is ever repressed by human error and sin.

Thus the actual church, the church as we see it here and now, seldom approximates the ideal church; but we cannot on that account write it off or leave it in disgust as a mere corruption. For within the actual church, however imperfect it may be, the "hidden force" of the ideal church struggles to realize itself. Hence if the visible church of history is not always perfect, it is always the true church; for it is the living body in which the ideal church struggles to realize its true nature, and its ministries are perennially valid.[38]

In terms of unity, Nevin continued, this means that the church, which is inwardly and ideally one, struggles to be visibly one and catholic. He called upon the denominations to apply themselves earnestly to that object by theological renewal and deep repentance over rampant sectarianism. It is, he said, "the most important interest in the world."[39]

SCHAFF'S PRINCIPLE OF PROTESTANTISM

In October 1844 the Synod of Allentown listened to Joseph Berg's sermon on the Waldensian origins of the German Reformed Church, with its overtones about a static orthodoxy brought down untainted from the blessed Polycarp.[40] Presently the Synod retired to Reading to hear the inaugural address of Philip Schaff, called "The Principle of Protestantism."[41] The Reformation, said Schaff, was "the legitimate offspring" and "greatest act" of the Catholic Church—the unfolding of the "true catholic nature itself."[42] With that, he laid bare to the astonished Synod his theory of historical development. That theory, like most vital theology through the ages, participated in current patterns of thought—including, we must admit, Hegelian categories. But Schaff did not deal with Hegel uncritically.[43]

By "development," Schaff did not infer that the church had undergone mere human improvement. On the contrary, Christianity, as the new order of life in Christ, was complete and perfect from the beginning. Thus "development" means an increasingly profound apprehension by the church of the life, doctrines, and spirit of Christ, and the assimilation of these into the course of catholic experience.[44] But even that does not occur by mere caprice, but by divine plan. As an ever-increasing stream, which flows its prescribed course; as a body, whose organic growth is regulated by an inner power; so the church moves out in history in a succession of great epochs, each building on the previous, according to providential direction.[45]

Schaff noted, in this connection, that the Reformers did not presume to reconstruct the great Catholic doctrines—the Trinity for instance, which had been perfected by the ecumenical councils. The concern of the Reformation lay chiefly in the realm of soteriology which had not been defined by such councils. Thus the doctrines of justification by faith and the final authority of the Bible involved no breach with Catholic life; on the contrary, those doctrines contributed to its fuller apprehension and articulation. In Schaff's words, the Reformation brought out "new scriptural statements without contradicting the true Catholic Church."[46]

He argued, with much evidence, that the entire Catholic Church pressed forward, by inward compulsion, toward the Reformation. The medieval church, with its legal and authoritarian structures, disciplined Christendom in its infancy, until such time as men were prepared for, and indeed demanded, the fuller appropriation of the evangelical principle and evangelical freedom. But the Reformers had no intention of overthrowing authority as such. Their object was rather to bind man over to the grace of God and to lead him captive to the Word of God. Nor did the Reformers ever concede the name Catholic or imagine themselves to be out of continuity with the ancient and medieval church. It was the Church of Rome that lost claim to catholicity by its fixation upon Romanism and therefore by its particularity.[47]

In the second part of his essay, where he discussed post-Reformation Christianity, Schaff dwelt upon the "diseases" of Protestantism, which he attributed to the growing exaggeration of the Protestant principle of freedom; and he saw that exaggeration to be an all too radical disjuncture with the Catholic principles of objectivity and authority. In the Reformation itself, evangelical freedom was held within its proper context, namely, in an objective church life which the Reformers intentionally brought over from the Middle Ages. But more and more that freedom ran out into self-will, private judgment, and endless subjectivism.

Schaff dealt chiefly with three of those diseases. Rationalism, the theoretical side of Protestant subjectivism, invaded especially the Lutheran Church of Germany. It beckoned to infidelity, to the disintegration of orthodox doctrine. Sectarianism, the practical side of the same subjectivism, overtook English-speaking Calvinism and lodged itself at the core of American Christianity. It was the principle of fragmentation which threatened to destroy more and more the corporate body of the church. The secularization of culture also owed its existence to a form of subjectivism, namely, the indifference of modern Protestantism to science, the arts, and government.

While the crisis of Protestantism was grave, Schaff did not despair, for he anticipated a new synthesis which he called "evangelical Catholicism." What did he intend by that? A mere appeal to the Bible, he said, will not be sufficient to stem the tide of subjectivism. What must now be asserted is the power of tradition and the right idea of the church as the mother of believers—all of this, he was careful to add, with due subordination always to the Word of God. Said Schaff: "The new life for Protestantism is to be secured through its full reconciliation with the objective idea of the church."[48]

Even there he would not stop, but prophesied the advent of a new epoch, the third age of Christianity, to be crowned by the ecumenical church. "A living outward intercommunion," he counseled, "must come to prevail among all Christian churches. . . . We may not exclude the Romanists themselves."[49] For neither

Protestantism nor Roman Catholicism can be consummated "until the truth of both tendencies be actualized as the power of one and the same life."[50]

Church history, he concluded, may be seen in three great stages. The first was the age of Peter, apostle of law and authority, and hence of Catholicism. The second was the age of Paul, apostle of grace and freedom, and thus of Protestantism. The third age, now impending, is the age of John, apostle of love who represents freedom *in* authority, and hence the final reconciliation of both communions. Schaff expected "this magnificent union," as he called it, to be wrought by the people of the New World in the nineteenth century.[51]

Granted the grandeur of Schaff's final proposal, we must not lose sight of the immediate import of his message to the little assembly of fathers and brethren at Reading. Having made certain that they saw the Reformation in its full catholic dimensions, he addressed a challenge to them which was eminently practical and eminently within their heritage, namely, to give evangelical catholicity a beginning within the German Reformed Church: "Let us labor then *within* our own denomination and *for* it, . . . knowing that God has given us here our own special commission to fulfill."[52]

CHARGES OF HERESY

Berg thought nothing of it. He hastened to publish *his* version of Reformed history under the title *The Old Paths*.[53] In sundry articles[54] he pointed to the "Romanizing tendencies" of Mercersburg and clung fiercely to the old ecclesiology. "The church," he said precisely, "does not make the believer. Believers constitute the church." Jacob Helffenstein ventured to say in the public press that Nevin and Schaff were really Tractarians—an unhappy allusion since John Henry Newman had by then decided for Rome.

Meanwhile the doctrine of the Eucharist had become entangled with the controversy. Berg printed the accusation that Nevin's doctrine of the spiritual real presence was "heresy," tainted by that mode of thought that leads logically to transubstantiation. In reply, Nevin informed Berg that the doctrine in question happened to be that of the Heidelberg Catechism, whereupon Berg threw off the historian's mantle and declared that at that point the Catechism was "absurd."[55]

In September 1845 the Classis of Philadelphia, under the management of Berg and four Helffensteins, drew up formal charges against the Mercersburg professors which were dispatched to the Synod.[56] When the Synod met at York in the fall of that year, the whole church was filled with intense excitement. Schaff was the defendant in the heresy trial, inasmuch as the charges, four of which pertained to the Eucharist, were made to rest on his inaugural essay. Berg proceeded to scrutinize the errors of Mercersburg; Nevin defended Schaff; Schaff defended himself. After four days of hearings, the Synod vindicated the professors by a vote of 40 to 7.[57]

THE MYSTICAL PRESENCE

That action did not for an instant resolve the controversy, which raged more and more over the question of the Lord's Supper. In June 1846 Nevin published his salient ideas on that subject in a monograph called *The Mystical Presence: A Vindication of the Reformed or Calvinistic Doctrine of the Holy Eucharist*. At the outset he advised his readers that the Lord's Supper was not only "the very heart of the whole Christian worship" but a doctrine which was profoundly related to one's idea of the church and to the character of one's churchmanship. It was scarcely an accident, then, that he spoke here for the first time about the "necessity" of "liturgical services."[58]

With copious evidence, Nevin documented the point that American Protestantism generally had fallen away from the sacramental doctrine of the sixteenth century and thus from the church system with which it was woven. The communities of Luther and Calvin, Wesley and Edwards had all become party to this vast defection. The grand idea of the day was the Zwinglian idea—which, Nevin maintained, had practically no authority in the entire history of Eucharistic theology. No one illustrated the predicament more poignantly than Nevin's own colleague, Berg, who said in 1846 that, Catechism or no, the Calvinist doctrine was irrelevant in American Christianity.

His chief object was to recover the sacramental theology of the classical Reformed confessions. This he proceeded to do by an extensive interpretation of the confessions themselves. Zwingli's historical influence he now discounted entirely. "It is not necessary," he said, "that we should trouble ourselves . . . about the opinions of Zwingli," whose relationship to the Reformed Church was "exceedingly external and accidental."[59] Reference must rather be made to Calvin whose view of the Lord's Supper acquired "general symbolical authority throughout the whole Reformed Church."[60] Nevin maintained that in the Heidelberg Catechism Calvin's doctrine is the one taught, in clear distinction to that of Zwingli.[61]

Finally Nevin offered a restatement of the Reformed doctrine based on certain amendments to Calvin's psychology. He commenced, characteristically, with a discussion of the Mystical Union which was the context in which he saw the Lord's Supper. Nevin insisted that justification by faith was more than a legal abstraction. Forensic justification could be brought home to the believer only by the Mystical Union, only by the actual sharing of Christ's life. And the Mystical Union, in turn, found its "epitome" in the Lord's Supper. He put it this way:

> The sacramental doctrine of the primitive Reformed Church stands inseparably connected with the idea of an inward, living union between the believers and Christ, in virtue of which they are incorporated into his very nature and made to subsist with him by the power of a common life. In full correspondence with this conception of the Christian salvation as a process by which the believer is mystically inserted more and more into the person of Christ, [the Reformed Church held that the proper use of the Lord's Supper required] nothing less than a real participation in his living person.[62]

Hence the purpose of the Lord's Supper was—and here Nevin quoted the Heidelberg Catechism—"to become more and more united to Christ's sacred body." When he came to the word body, he was concerned to amend Calvin's psychology[63]—at a point where perhaps it did not need amending. What, he asked, gives identity to a body? Certainly not its chemical properties which are apt to shift hourly and which do not in any case constitute a system of life. That which gives identity to a body is its "living force," its "animating power"—what Calvin apparently meant by the expression "vivific virtue of Christ's flesh." Thus, to feed upon the matter of Christ's body would be of no value. What really happens in the sacrament is that the "animating power" of Christ's life is brought over into the very center of our persons by the agency of the Holy Spirit. It is not taken by mouth, but received by faith. It is not bound locally to the bread and wine, but to the act of eating and drinking in the sacramental mystery as a whole.

Nevin insisted, as did Calvin, upon the objective power of the sacrament. Its virtue is not put into it by the faith of the worshiper, nor made to disappear by a corresponding lack of faith. Its power is objective and divine, rooted in God's promise to have communion with his people in this stated way. Yet the efficacy of the sacrament to the communicant, whether or not he will receive it to his benefit, does indeed depend entirely upon his faith.[64]

CONTINUED OPPOSITION

Nearly two years passed before any new blow was struck at the Mercersburg theology. However, in 1848, *The Mystical Presence* was fairly dismantled in the *Princeton Review*. Nevin's critic was the celebrated Charles Hodge of Princeton Seminary, spokesman of the Old School Presbyterians. Hodge observed that he had allowed the book to gather dust for two years—it pained him so to read about such doctrines. Nevin, he said, was a promising fellow, but he had read the evidence the wrong way. There were, in fact, three views of the Supper taught in the Reformed confessions: that of Zwingli, that of Calvin, and a third which somehow skittered between the two and must in the last analysis be classified Zwinglian. To the third category he consigned the Heidelberg Catechism.

The point of Hodge's historical case was to bring confessional support to the Zwinglian view, with which he found himself sympathetic. But, according to Hodge, Nevin's trouble did not stop at history. His view of justification was Romanist. He hearkened too much to Schleiermacher and was therefore short on sin and long on liturgy. He had harnessed the Holy Spirit by asserting the objective potency of the Lord's Supper. And so on and on. Besides, said Hodge, the high sacramental interest which Nevin professed was incompatible with the real center of Reformed theology, namely, God's absolute decrees.

Nevin was stung. Through the summer of 1848 he stuffed *The Messenger* with rebuttal, until the subscribers complained that even what they could understand they were weary of. Nevin applied to the theological journals, but they refused his pieces. Hence the Alumni Association of Marshall College resolved to commence the *Mercersburg Review*, which made its appearance in 1849. In the second volume of that journal, over the course of 128 pages, Nevin gave the sum of his reply to Hodge.[65] Here the historical ground was painstakingly removed from Hodge's position until he was left standing with such notables as Carlstadt. (Nevin was tickled by the possibility that not even Ulrich Zwingli was a conventional Zwinglian.) After that no word was heard from Princeton about the classic Reformed doctrine of the Lord's Supper.

Hodge left one lasting impression on Nevin. He convinced him that Calvin's doctrine of the decrees was finally incompatible with Calvin's sacramental interest. This Nevin conceded in 1850[66]; it is but one indication of his inability (or lack of training) to fathom Calvin fully. At any rate, he maneuvered to meet the problem. Melanchthon, he noted, rejected Calvin's doctrine of the decrees as "a metaphysical abstraction" yet agreed in the main with Calvin's view of the Supper. Was not the gentle Melanchthon the real father of the German Reformed Church?[67] And through his pupil, Ursinus, did not the Melanchthonian spirit come to "pervade every page . . . of the Heidelberg Catechism"?[68]

By this line of reasoning Nevin could draw the desirable conclusion: "The doctrine of the decrees, as held by Calvin, never belonged to the constitution of the [German] Reformed Church, . . . whereas the sacramental doctrine [of Calvin and Melanchthon] entered into its distinctive character as a confession."[69] There was truth in this Melanchthonian hypothesis, although Nevin tended to overstate it.

So by his labors, Nevin recovered the Reformed doctrine of the Eucharist, exalted the authority of the Heidelberg Catechism, laid the theological groundwork for the Mercersburg liturgy, and proposed the thesis that the worship of the ecumenical church has a Eucharistic center. James H. Nichols[70] and Howard G. Hageman[71] both deplore the fact that the Mercersburg theology did not also involve a recovery of preaching, especially as Calvin could not have been more explicit about the proper relationship of the Word in sermon and sacrament. It is a fair criticism. We may at least say to ourselves that a high doctrine of preaching is not alien to the Mercersburg tradition, but is virtually demanded by it.

THE HEIDELBERG CATECHISM

In 1846, prior to the fight with Hodge, Nevin assembled and edited his articles on the Catechism which had been published some years before in *The Messenger*. They made up a little book called *The History and Genius of the Heidelberg Catechism*.[72] The two final chapters were newly written. In the first of these[73] Nevin treated the theology of the Catechism in a popular fashion, but was careful to note the points at which it corresponded to Mercersburg teachings. He expressed satisfaction that the Catechism did not involve the speculative predestinarianism from which he himself had lately drawn away and against which he and Schaff were quite self-consciously developing their theology. In Questions 20, 32, and 64, he claimed confirmation for his views on justification and the Mystical Union; and to the questions on the Lord's Supper he found himself entirely congenial.

In sum, Nevin declared that the Catechism comprehended, without much particularity, the faith commonly held by what he called "the Catholic Church Reformed." Here the evangelical principle seemed to be preserved side by side with an objective, historical, catholic spirit.

In the final chapter he dealt specifically with the "church spirit" of the Catechism.[74] At last he had found someone who knew something about the Palatinate Liturgy. A copy had turned up at Easton, and Bomberger had sent a digest of it to Mercersburg. Nevin seemed astonished at what he discovered in the old Church Order—which leads one to suspect that never before had he quite understood that dimension in Calvin's thought which laid stress upon the *visible* church and thereby furnished the basis for a high degree of churchmanship. So this, Nevin exclaimed, was the shape of the Reformed Church "before the flood"![75]

Here he found the Catechism set within the context of a baptismal-educational religion, informed by sound preaching and catechetical instruction; stimulated by parochial discipline; furnished by simple yet decidedly liturgical worship, with a stated service for the Lord's Day, *monthly* communion, and a high doctrine of baptismal grace. Here, said Nevin, the church is understood to be "the medium and bearer of spiritual life for her . . . children. . . .One thing is certain," he concluded with fresh defiance, "the German Church is not Puritan."[76]

THE MERCERSBURG LITURGY

Nevin's book on the Catechism evidently made an impression. In 1847 the Synod received an overture from the East Pennsylvania Classis to print the Palatinate Liturgy or draft another in "the spirit of our Catechism."[77] There being little unanimity among the Classes over the matter, it was referred to a committee headed by J. H. A. Bomberger,[78] who was something of an expert on the Palatinate Church Order.

To the Synod of 1849, Bomberger proposed the preparation of a liturgy, along the lines of the Palatinate formulary, which would represent liturgical, not free, worship, and would therefore include a form for the Lord's Day. In the ensuing debate, Samuel Helffenstein inquired whether the liturgy would be high or low. Bomberger replied, medium—a fair estimate of his own liturgical position. His proposals were adopted, however, with high unanimity. Nevin was given charge of the Liturgical Committee.[79]

According to the opinions which Nevin and Schaff had expressed in their writings, they were not apt to be content with a mere reproduction of the old Palatinate book. They agreed that a liturgy was not simply a convenience to the church, nor an aid to decency and order. It was the sum of other things: the expression of doctrine, the voice of the catholic church at worship, the guarantor against arbitrary freedom, the instrument of the common priesthood, and an art form which expresses the spirit of communal worship. We desired, said Schaff, "a scriptural, historical, evangelical Catholic" liturgy for the people as well as for the ministry.[80]

But Nevin was doubtful. What profit would it be to furnish such a liturgy to a church which lacked a liturgical spirit? As early as 1848 he predicted failure.[81] The committee, under his direction, evaded a decision; and in 1851 he resigned the chairmanship as well as his professorship, owing to his inhuman load of responsibilities and to the theological uncertainty into which he had fallen.

Schaff was appointed chairman; and even in the face of Nevin's hopelessness, he was ardent for the task. He had seen the liturgical renewal succeed in Germany.[82] And he far exceeded Nevin in the knowledge of liturgical literature. Now earnestly at work, the committee reviewed the great catholic rites, arrived at a general plan for the new book, and agreed upon principles of procedures.[83]

These activities were duly reported to the Synod of Baltimore in 1852.[84] The principles, in particular, involved some extraordinary innovations. As the "general basis" of the new liturgy, the committee proposed to refer to "the liturgical worship of the primitive church" as far as that could be ascertained from the Scriptures and the ancient Greek and Latin rites. "Special reference" would then be given to the Palatinate and other orders of the Reformed Church. None of the liturgies was to be reproduced slavishly, but "in a free evangelical spirit," in the language and style of scripture, and without the didactic tyranny of the early Reformed rites. It would be decidedly a people's liturgy, for home and pew, to enhance genuinely corporate worship and to discourage the excursions of ministers. Into the liturgy would be woven the church year, with a complete lectionary and festival prayers for the great seasons.

The minutes of the Synod of Baltimore state with eloquent clarity: "The report was adopted and the Committee [was] continued."[85] Thus did the German Reformed Church set its sanction to a document which established the shape and spirit of the Mercersburg liturgical tradition, and gave reality for the first time to the evangelical Catholic principle.

Such was the formative period of the Mercersburg theology: its celebrities and books, its doctrines and liturgy, and the church out of which it arose.

CONCLUSION

How true were the Mercersburg divines to the Heidelberg Catechism and the Palatinate Liturgy? We could argue that they were far more responsible to those standards than their opponents were. We could surely maintain that they renewed their church, despite the desperate struggles which pursued their efforts. But such assertions do not really answer the question.

The Mercersburg theology was a twofold procedure: recovery and progress. We must not underestimate the genuine conservatism of Nevin and Schaff. They attempted to recover the Reformation in its catholic dimensions, the Reformed doctrine of the Eucharist, the stature of the Heidelberg Catechism, the liturgical basis of Reformed worship, the sense of Reformed churchmanship. To the American church as a whole, they opened a vast new historical perspective. Yet for the following reasons they deemed recovery to be insufficient.

First, theology itself must be alive to the moment. Said Nevin: "To be . . . living and vigorous, our theology must be more than traditional. It must keep pace with the onward course of human thought. . . . Theology *must* advance . . . to conquer, or die."[86] In his sermon "Catholic Unity," Nevin advocated a "republication of the principles of the Reformation, not in the letter that killeth, . . . but by entering with free and profound insight into that faith itself."[87] All of this was self-evident to Nevin and Schaff who found themselves, not peering over Ursinus' shoulder as he wrote the Catechism, but standing on the other side of rationalism, and sectarianism, in the midst of "pseudo-Protestantism."

Second, Protestantism itself meant movement. "Puseyism looks backward," Schaff remarked, "we look forward. . . . We move toward Jerusalem, the new, the heavenly, the eternal."[88] This principle of movement had its impulse in Schaff's historical thought, and in Nevin's doctrine of the ideal and actual church. It was impelled particularly by the whole Mercersburg thrust toward an evangelical Catholicism and, finally, the age of the ecumenical church. "Protestantism," said Schaff in explaining the title of his inaugural essay, "is the principle of movement, of progress in the history of the church; progress, not such as may go beyond the Bible and Christianity, but such as consists in an ever-extending knowledge of the Bible itself, and an ever-deepening appropriation of Christianity as the power of a divine life which is destined to make all things new."[89]

Hendrikus Berkhof

•

THE CATECHISM IN HISTORICAL CONTEXT

THE CATECHISM AS AN EXPRESSION OF OUR FAITH

HENDRIKUS BERKHOF is professor of Biblical Theology and Dogmatics at the University of Leiden.

CHAPTER FOUR

The Catechism in Historical Context

IN THE YEAR 1559, on the twelfth of February, Otto Heinrich, Elector of the Palatinate, died childless. So it was that Germany's richest principality came under the hegemony of the ruling house of Simmern represented by Frederick III, who thereafter moved his residence from Kaiserslautern to Heidelberg, the capital of the Electorate. Otto Heinrich had successfully reorganized the church and had established the Reformation in its Lutheran form. Frederick also was deeply committed to the Reformation as was his Lutheran wife, Maria of Brandenburg-Bayreuth.

AN IRENIC ATMOSPHERE

The spirit in which the Reformation in the Palatinate had started and developed in its first phase, was that of the peaceful Philip Melanchthon who, coming from the Palatinate himself, exercised an important influence and assisted with frequent advice. One of his suggestions was to appoint as the general-superintendent of the church his pupil Tilemann Hesshus. This man, to the disappointment of his teacher and many others, turned out to be a fanatic Lutheran who was inclined to remove by force every deviation from the Lutheran doctrine and practice of the Lord's Supper. His reformation of the existing liturgy was of such a nature that it seemed to the majority to be a return to transubstantiation.

The Catechism in Historical Context

A heavy conflict broke out as a consequence, which had reached a climax when Frederick became Elector. He removed Hesshus for his quarrelsomeness, and consulted Melanchthon. The latter proposed a liturgy and a form for the celebration of the Holy Supper which might satisfy all parties.

Frederick arranged a debate in Heidelberg between Lutheran theologians and some who were inclined to the Reformation in the form in which it was presented by men like Henry Bullinger and John Calvin. The pious Elector was won for the latter group because, as he said, its arguments were more biblical. He decided therefore to carry out the Reformation along the lines of its "Reformed" manifestation. His wife remained a Lutheran. He himself was of an irenic nature, sharing that spirit with Melanchthon. Consequently he created in the Palatinate an atmosphere which was at the same time Reformed and open for union with the Lutherans. It was a veritable ecumenical atmosphere whose wholesome influence was felt throughout centuries and continents.

A NEW CATECHISM

The Heidelberg Catechism was the reason for this remarkable influence. In 1562 Frederick took the initiative in creating a catechism for the Electorate. He personally appreciated Luther's Small Catechism. But it had been involved in the recent conflict and, besides, was too brief for the ideals of national religious education which the Elector pursued. The charge to compose a catechism was primarily given to 28-year-old Zacharias Ursinus who had been born in Breslau.

In September of 1561 this gifted scholar had accepted an appointment to the chair of dogmatics at the University of Heidelberg and the leadership of the Collegium Sapientiae, a kind of *Predigerseminar*. In the interests of religious instruction in the Collegium Sapientiae he had already written a catechism, *Summa Theologiae,* better known as the *Catechesis Maior*. This work bore the stamp of Calvin but also at its center had the conception of the covenant which was so characteristic of Ursinus' teacher Bullinger. The *Catechesis* consisted of two parts: "Law and Gospel." The first question reads: "What is your firm comfort in life and in death?" The essential words of the long answer are: "That God . . . out of his immense and gratuitous mercy has taken me into the covenant of his grace . . . and that he has sealed this his own covenant in my heart by his Spirit . . . and by his Word and the visible signs of this covenant."[1]

This catechism, of course, was too long and too theological for the rank and file Palatine people. So Ursinus made a smaller one called the *Catechesis Minor*. While the *Maior* has 323 questions, the *Minor* has 108. The idea of the covenant as central is replaced by that of comfort which was already dominant, as seen in the first question of the *Maior*. Now Question 1 reads: "What is your comfort to which your heart holds in death as well as in life?" The answer is: "That God has certainly forgiven all my sins for Christ's sake and has granted me eternal life in which I shall praise him forever."[2] The third question asks: "What does the Word of God teach?" And the answer reads: "First, it shows us our misery; further, how we shall be liberated from it; and what gratitude we have to show to God for this liberation."[3] Here we first find the famous tripartite composition of the catechism.

In the *Minor* the entire material is reshaped from the point of view of popular religious instruction. A reduction and limitation to the essential biblical and devotional elements has taken place. Thus the typical Calvinistic questions about eternal reprobation —53 and 54 of the *Maior*—are removed.

Between this *Catechesis Minor* and our Heidelberg Catechism there is no essential difference, but there are many differences in detail. In some cases elements of the *Maior* are taken up anew; in many other cases concentration on the biblical and devotional aspect of truth has been extended. The popular accent has been strengthened, especially by the translation from the Latin to the German.

AUTHORS OF THE HEIDELBERG CATECHISM

Who did this work? It seems impossible that Ursinus himself rephrased his work in this way. Here the name of Caspar Olevianus comes to mind. Born at Olewig near Trier, Olevianus came to the chair of dogmatics at Heidelberg and the leadership of the Collegium Sapientiae in 1560, when he was twenty-four. (He was the predecessor of Ursinus.) Not being a scholar, however, but rather a great preacher, pastor, and church administrator—he created the famous Palatinate Church Order—he went back to the ministry in 1561.

It is still commonly thought that Ursinus and Olevianus together made the Heidelberg Catechism. This is due to Henry Alting whose *Historia Ecclesiastica Palatina* was for long our main source of information for this period. Alting writes:

> Each one put his draft on paper: Olevianus, a popular explanation of the covenant of grace; Ursinus, two works—a major catechism for advanced students and a minor one for beginners. Out of both was contracted the Palatine Catechism which because of its birthplace is customarily called the Heidelberg Catechism.[4]

This statement cannot be correct. Ursinus did not make the *Maior* as a draft for the Heidelberg Catechism and Olevianus did not make any draft at all. We know that Olevianus cooperated in the work, but we have no evidence of his contribution. So it is understandable that some have minimized his part in the work. But Alting cannot have mentioned him together with Ursinus without good reason. Moreover we know no one who was so capable of giving the Catechism its popular tone and its devotional warmth as Olevianus. The opinion, therefore, that Ursinus contributed the content and Olevianus the form may still hold good.

Nevertheless it is a remarkable fact that in the oldest testimonies Ursinus and Olevianus are nowhere mentioned as authors. Ursinus himself speaks in his *Apologia Catechismi* about a commission given to some teachers who were famous for their experience in Christian doctrine. He speaks as if he did not belong to that group himself. Olevianus writes to Calvin (April 3, 1563): "If the Catechism is approved by you in every respect, those who have collected the thoughts which are expressed in it will be satisfied." And in a letter to Theodore Beza he writes: "I send these booklets to you in the name of us all." These utterances give the impression that the Catechism is the work of a whole group of persons. This supposition is in accordance with the words written by the Elector in the preface to the first edition:

So we have instructed to write and compose a short instruction or catechism of our Christian religion out of the Word of God, both in the German and the Latin languages with the advice and co-operation (*mit Rat und Zuthun*) of our whole theological faculty here and also of all superintendents and the most important ministers of the church.[5]

In a very scholarly work a Dutch professor, M. A. Gooszen, has proved it probable that this statement is correct and that the Catechism is the result of a broad cooperation.[6]

Though it is likely that Olevianus was the leading spirit in the final redaction, we have reason to assume that many others made proposals and corrections. Among these must have been men like the court preacher Michael Diller and the lay member of the upper church council, Thomas Erastus, who in the same year 1562 wrote a booklet on the Lord's Supper. It is not less probable that the Elector himself, with his passion for the religious education of his people, took an active part in the last phase of the phrasing. But we cannot say more because of lack of data.

Some presume that Frederick himself was the author of the famous first answer which is so strikingly similar to his wonderful confession of faith in a letter of June 10, 1562.[7] This confession looks like a broad paraphrase of the first answer. But we do not know what the connection between the two is or even whether there is a connection at all. Both could be due to the broad and warm Reformed devotion which was dominant in the Palatinate at that time. With greater certainty we can assume that either Frederick or the Synod which approved the Catechism slightly changed Question 78 about the real presence of Christ in the Holy Supper. This was probably done to avoid the impression that bread and wine would be a mere resemblance or image, i.e., to avoid the Zwinglian doctrine.

The preface of the Elector in the first edition ends with the words: "Given at Heidelberg on Tuesday the nineteenth day of the month January, in the year one thousand five hundred sixty-three after the birth of Christ our dear Lord and Savior."[8] What does this date mean? Alting says, "When the catechetical booklet was completed and shown to the Elector he called together at

The Catechism in Historical Context

Heidelberg the principal Palatine inspectors and pastors when the year was already coming to its end (*anno iam declinante*) and gave the booklet to them to be reviewed."[9] On that statement the widespread opinion has been built that the Catechism was given its definite form and was approved in the month of December 1562. The nineteenth of January, in that case, must have been the day on which the Catechism was published or given to the press. But the correspondence after the offering of the Catechism to princes and Reformers makes it probable that the Catechism was not published earlier than February.

In the library at Weimar is a pamphlet about the Heidelberg Catechism which has an important marginal note about the preceding Synod. It reads:

> To give another confirmation (i.e., of the acceptance of the Catechism), they went to the Holy Supper on Sunday the seventeenth of January together with the Concessors.* On the eighteenth of January the Elector summoned them to the chancery and spoke thus: "We have heard from the Concessors that you have given your unanimous consent, which pleases us highly. We desire from you to observe it faithfully."[10]

The date of the preface is in accordance with this statement. So I assume that this date indicates the end of the Synod and the release of the Catechism for printing (as is also suggested by the preface of the fourth edition, in the Church Order of the Palatinate[11]). If this supposition is correct, Alting has dated the Synod incorrectly (unless we have to suppose that the words *anno iam declinante* indicate the period in which Frederick sent out the call for the convocation of the Synod).

THE PURPOSE OF THE CATECHISM

From the beginning the Heidelberg Catechism had a threefold purpose: it was meant as a catechism for the youth, as a guide for preaching, and as a creedal statement. The first editions were in some aspects different from that which we have now, i.e., the fourth edition of November 1563. They had no division into Sundays or enumeration of questions. The Catechism had to be

---

* The representatives of the elector.

read in nine parts in services held on Sunday mornings. In the afternoon service the preacher had to treat the Catechism so that he covered it in fifty-two times. The fourth edition gave these divisions, but not yet the numbering of the questions. At the end of the Catechism a summary was given which had to be read at every afternoon service.

Far more important than the slight additions already mentioned is the fact that the first edition had one question less than we have now: Question 80 with its renowned rejection of the idolatry of the Roman Mass was missing. The second edition added it in a form which was slightly different from and less sharp than the text which we now have, since the third edition has an extension of three phrases. Much has been written to explain the insertion of this question. The second edition gives an explanation on the last page: *"An den christlichen Leser. Was im ersten Druck übersehen, als fürnemlich folio 55, ist jetzunder auss befelch churfürstlicher Gnaden addiert worden. 1563."* This explanation raised suspicions. It looked contradictory. If something is simply overlooked, why does it need a formal order of the Elector to be added?

Nevertheless Olevianus in his letter to Calvin on April 3, 1563, writes exactly the same in these words: "In the first German edition . . . the question about the difference between the Lord's Supper and the papal Mass was omitted. Admonished by me the Prince desired that it should be added in the second German and in the first Latin edition." And the national library in Vienna has a copy of the Catechism with a page pasted in, containing Question 80.

So we have good reason to believe that the official explanation is correct. But we do not know the motives. Was this a mere omission in the synodical deliberation and was the drafted text quickly inserted? Then we can suppose that the extension in the third edition was a revision after further deliberation. Or did it suddenly come to the mind of Olevianus that the authors had skipped an important question? In that case many presume that in the period after the close of the Synod the Tridentine decree about the sacrifice of the Mass (*decretum de sacrificio missae*) of September 17, 1562 had become known in Germany and demanded a clear answer. The so-called *Rekusationsschrift* of 1561 proves the great attention with which the German Protestant princes and theologians followed the decisions of the Council of Trent. This explanation seems the most probable to me also. But we have no proof and we know even less why the answer was extended and sharpened in the third edition.

In the seventeenth century when the Palatinate came under a Roman prince, the Jesuits took the words "accursed idolatry" (*vermaledeite Abgötterey*) as a reason for their restless attempts to rule the Reformed confession out of the protection of the Treaty of Augsburg of 1555.

REACTIONS TO THE CATECHISM

The Heidelberg Catechism caused many widespread reactions. The quick succession of editions and the different translations show how gratefully this booklet was received in the world of the Reformation, in the schools and in the families, as well as in the churches. I have even read somewhere that in an area of persecution an edition was published which was so small that children could hide it in their footwear. Bullinger, in Zurich, was so enthusiastic that he wrote:

> The composition of this book is clear and its content is pure truth. All is very understandable, pious, fruitful; in concise brevity it contains a fullness of the most important doctrines. I consider it to be the best catechism ever published. God be praised; may he crown it with his blessing.[12]

This appraisal is still to the point.

In letters to Beza and Calvin, Bullinger recommended that the Catechism be translated into French. What was Calvin's opinion? This is mysterious. In July 1563 he dedicated his commentary on Jeremiah to Frederick III, whom he praises for his sound doctrine of the Holy Table. But he is silent about the Catechism though it was sent to him by Olevianus as early as April. We have no utterance at all by Calvin about our Catechism. What can the reason be?

We have indications that shortly before, in 1561, Calvin did not welcome the publication of Guido de Brès' *Confessio Belgica* because he judged it better that the Netherlands accept the *Confessio Gallicana* of their French brethren for which Calvin had written the draft. Something similar is probably true here. It is possible that Calvin disagreed with the creation of new confessional and catechetical works and felt that his own Catechism of Geneva would meet the educational needs and ideals of the Elector. But this is mere hypothesis. If that really was Calvin's feeling he could have known that he had a wrong impression of the situation in the Palatinate because Olevianus in his letter of April 3 had told him frankly that Ursinus had translated the Catechism of Geneva but had omitted the names of Calvin and Genève, "to avoid having the Germans refuse to read it" (*ne Germani lectionem recusent*). Olevianus had also hoped, as he writes, that the concept of the Catechism would be submitted to Calvin, "but strange tricks were put in the way. So difficult is it to reconcile many heads and to bring them together." Then the closing words of the letter follow: "Good-bye. Respond with one word."

That one word never came and we can only speculate as to why Calvin showed no interest in the Heidelberg Catechism. At the same time these rather unknown words of Olevianus are important for two reasons. First, they affirm what has been said about the broad cooperation (and sometimes even opposition) which lies behind the Catechism. Second, they show that both Ursinus and Olevianus were convinced that they edited a book in full accordance with the mind of Calvin. In spite of Calvin's silence the Catechism found a quick acceptance in the Reformed churches in Germany, Switzerland, Hungary, the Netherlands, and later in South Africa and North America, and in many Reformed minority groups all over the world.

But the Catechism also encountered strong resistance. From the very beginning right-wing Lutherans attacked it heavily, especially on the point of the Lord's Supper. The Catechism was accused of deviation from the *Augustana Variata*, of Zwinglianism, of considering the elements of the sacrament not as organs of grace but as mere signs. As early as May 1563, three Lutheran princes (of Zweibrücken, Württemberg, and Baden) sent a long letter of warning to Frederick accompanied by an indication of the errors in the Heidelberg Catechism. This was the so-called

The Catechism in Historical Context

Anweisung. Frederick III, supported by his theologians, answered in a letter of September 14, 1563, in which he wrote that he had never read one letter of Zwingli or of Calvin but that he considered his catechism to be in full accordance with holy scripture. He emphasized also its agreement with the *Variata* because the Heidelberg Catechism believes in the real presence of Christ and sees the elements in the Supper as organs of that presence.

New attacks came. At the end of 1563 the *Widerlegung* of Matthias Flacius, and in the spring of 1564 the *Treue Warnung* of the Elector's old enemy, Hesshus, appeared. Ursinus answered both booklets in the first half of 1564 in his *Gründlicher Bericht*.

In these theological discussions important political consequences were also at stake. It was doubtful whether Frederick's government could be considered as protected by the peace treaty of Augsburg concluded in 1555 between the Catholics and the Lutherans. It is shameful to see how bitterly one part of the Reformation behaved itself toward another even in that time of utmost struggle for life. At the Imperial Diet at Augsburg in 1566 Frederick had to defend his catechism and he did it in a most brilliant and impressive way. The main trend of his defense was somewhat as follows: I am open for correction and revocation if anyone can prove that my catechism is against the Scriptures!

For good reason the attitude of Frederick at Augsburg has been compared with that of Martin Luther at Worms. His words made a deep impression. The danger blew over. The Elector of Saxony expressed the mood of many others present when he slapped Frederick on the shoulder and said, *"Fritz, du bist frömmer als wir alle!"*

THE CATECHISM AND THE REFORMATION

Turning from the external story of the Catechism, we now focus our attention on the question: What is the place of the Catechism in the catechetical and dogmatical evolution of the first decades of the Reformation?

Catechetical Aspect

In the Middle Ages the Christian education of baptized children was centered around, or limited to, three subjects: learning by heart the Apostles' Creed, the Ten Commandments, and the Lord's Prayer—succinctly called in German *Glaube, Gebot, Gebet*. As on so many other points, here also the Reformation was linked with the tradition from which it came. But there were from the beginning two remarkable alterations: new subjects were added to the explanation of the Creed, i.e., justification by faith, faith and works, and the sacraments. And according to the new conception of faith, the first authors of catechisms attempted to concentrate the various data of the catechetical material under one head. Thus Calvin in his Catechism of Geneva (1541) derived the material from the true knowledge and worship of God.

Bullinger in his *Summa Christenlicher Religion* (1556) and Ursinus in his *Catechesis Maior* (1561) subsumed the catechetical elements under the conception of the covenant. Perhaps it is better to say that these three attempted to concentrate the material, for their work did not lead to a significant reshaping of the catechism.

The real reformation of the catechetical tradition was reserved to Ursinus in his creation of the Heidelberg Catechism. Here the triple composition of the older catechisms—Creed, Law, Prayer—is preserved but at the same time taken into a new context, i.e., a context of Misery, Redemption, and Gratitude. The Creed is subsumed under Redemption; the Law, partly under Misery and mainly under Gratitude; the Prayer, under Gratitude. This tripartite composition transfers the whole content of faith from the sphere of objective credenda in which it had been located for centuries to the sphere of personal confession, decision, and action. This wonderful composition reveals a man of religious and theological genius. Here a new and highly adequate hermeneutical key was given to open the riches of divine revelation and to show both the catholicity and the existentiality of the Christian faith. It is no wonder that many have tried to discover the origin of this illuminating presentation of the faith. Henry Alting wrote:

> The method of the Catechism is analytical, in accordance with the disposition of Paul in the letter to the Romans; for first the end is presented, i.e., the Christian comfort, Romans 1:16-17; next are laid down the necessary means to obtain it, three in number: in

the recognition of our misery, chapters 1—3; of our deliverance, from 3:23 until chapter 12; and of our gratitude, from chapter 12 until the end.[13]

So Alting considers the order of the Catechism as an imitation of the order of the letter to the Romans. But Philip Schaff rightly remarks that this at any rate cannot have been a conscious imitation, because under the nine Bible references which are mentioned in the first editions as evidence for Answer 2, there is but one passage from the letter to the Romans, i.e., Romans 6, mentioned in connection with gratitude.[14] Others believe that the disposition of Melanchthon's *Loci Communes* (first edition) was the guide for the authors of the Catechism. But one look at the division of the *Loci* shows us that this explanation is not convincing either. The same can be said about the newly undertaken attempt to seek the origins in two confessions made by Beza.[15]

Nowhere is this tripartite composition so clear and central and so determinative of the whole material as in the Catechism of Heidelberg. It is true that the mind of the Reformed confession, deeply influenced by the letter to the Romans and emphasizing the positive use of the Law more than the Lutherans, pressed toward this total and existential approach to the faith. The liturgy which was written in Strassburg under the leadership of Martin Bucer and which was used by Calvin also has in principle the division: confession of sin, announcement of grace, reading of the Law as a rule for our obedience. But I repeat, the systematic and consequent use of this approach is the original discovery of Ursinus. Its practicality endures down the centuries. It has demonstrated itself to be a guide to find the existential and well-balanced answer in many theological and pastoral problems.

Much effort has been made to show the coherence of the Catechism in content and details with other Reformed catechisms published in former years, especially the two catechisms of Leo Judae (1533, 1535), the *Summa* of Bullinger, the Catechism of Geneva, and the catechisms of the Netherlands refugee churches in London and Emden that in 1562 fled to the Palatinate. Especially M. A. Gooszen, August Lang, and James I. Good have done important work in this field.[16] But the result is rather meager. Or better, these comparisons confirm the high originality and the spiritual depth of the Heidelberg Catechism which stands unrivaled in the midst of the rich Reformed catechetical literature and on the highest summits of catechetical literature in general.

The Heidelberg Catechism has only one disadvantage: it is too difficult for children to understand and learn. We are used to saying it is antiquated from a pedagogical point of view. But it was difficult even for the children of the Reformation era. Therefore in 1585 the Palatine Elector John Casimir published "the little Heidelberg Catechism," which is a simple and popular extract of the original. In the introduction the Elector declares that "various questions in the large catechism seem to be too long or too difficult for the common man and for the youth."

Dogmatical Significance

In the nineteenth century certain scholars defended the thesis that the Heidelberg Catechism represents neither a Lutheran nor a Calvinistic type of thinking, but a third style. This *tertium genus* is supposedly the *genre* of German-speaking Switzerland, of Ulrich Zwingli and particularly of Henry Bullinger and his covenant theology. This style over against that of Calvin was defined as antischolastic and biblical-soteriological. It is evident that the Catechism breathes an atmosphere different from that of the French-speaking Reformers. We know that Ursinus was specially attached to his teacher Bullinger and, as we have already noted, his *Catechesis Maior* had the concept of the covenant at its center. We know also that Bullinger had grave objections to Calvin's doctrine of eternal reprobation and that this doctrine is not found in the Catechism, in which even predestination in general hardly has a place.

Nevertheless the hypothesis of a *tertium genus* and of the Heidelberg Catechism as one of its fruits has no foundation in fact. First, because the Reformers, who by this theory are placed on two sides of a divide, belonged together in their own idea or in the appreciation of their followers. In spite of many differences the correspondence between Bullinger and Calvin is between good friends. Ursinus was attached to Bullinger but, as we have heard, he also made a translation of Calvin's Catechism. And Olevianus considered himself even more a student of Calvin. The Catechism was sent to Calvin and Beza as well as to Bullinger and the authors expected the approval of them all.

This general observation is confirmed by the situation involving the touchy doctrine of the Lord's Supper. Since the *Consensus Tigurinus,* Zurich and Geneva no longer had basic differences on that point. The Heidelberg Catechism has no inclination to Zwinglianism. On the contrary, the authors and the Elector tried to formulate the presence of Christ at his table in such a way that accord with the *Variata* would be evident. So it necessarily expresses far more the view of Calvin than that of Bullinger, let alone that of Zwingli. Far from representing a left-wing type of statement the Catechism tried to build a bridge toward the Lutheran confession. We deplore the fact that Answers 47 and 48 about the two natures of Christ definitely frustrated a mutual understanding. But these answers are also entirely in the line of Calvin's thought. Moreover, as has been said, in 1563 Calvin praised the Elector for his sound conception of the Holy Supper.

Things look different in the field of predestination. The Catechism seems to be silent about what is often considered the central dogma of Calvinism. The concept is only mentioned in connection with the church in Answer 54: "a congregation chosen for eternal life" (*eine auszerwelte Gemein zum ewigen Leben*). The word election is not used for the individual. This does not mean that the notion itself is lacking. Answer 54 ends with the words "I am and forever will remain a living member of it," which confession strongly expresses the Reformed doctrine of the perseverance of the saints by God's electing grace. The same can be said about the doctrine of regeneration in Question 8: "Are we so perverted that we are altogether unable to do good and prone to do evil? Yes, unless we are born again through the Spirit of God."

There is, as a matter of fact, no word about eternal reprobation. But that does not prove anything. It is an error to consider this dogma as the identification mark of Calvin's reformation. Only as late as 1559, in the last edition of the *Institutes,* does Calvin give his broad treatment of predestination, moved by what he considered to be grave errors about it. In his Catechism of

Geneva he speaks, or rather, he is silent about predestination in the same way as is the Catechism of Heidelberg.

Moreover, Ursinus, so attached to Bullinger, wrote in his *Catechesis Maior* two questions about reprobation which hardly can have pleased his teacher, but were typically Calvinistic. God governs the wicked, Answer 53 says, "so that they cannot even move without his will but he neither sanctifies nor leads them by his grace and Spirit." But in the *Catechesis Minor* this thought has disappeared. And Olevianus has left it out also in the final form of the Heidelberg Catechism. These eloquent facts prove anew that eternal reprobation was a theologoumenon at the fringe of the Reformed faith which could be denied or omitted without splitting the unity of faith.

Therefore we have not the slightest reason to ascribe the Catechism to a particular trend in the Reformed tradition. The omission of eternal reprobation had no dogmatical, but pedagogical, reasons as Philip Schaff, August Lang, and others have rightly pointed out. Calvin himself shrank from this doctrine and exclaimed, "I acknowledge, it is a horrible decree!" *(Institutes* 3: 23:7) He did not like to teach it to the children.

One can ask with good reason whether a doctrine is sound that cannot be taught in a simple way to children. Personally I believe that the Reformed theologoumenon is a transgression of the limits which are placed around the knowledge of faith. The Netherlands Reformed Church has published a declaration on the doctrine of election in which one of the conclusions is that the personal and positive, and at the same time restrained and indirect, way in which this doctrine is treated in the Heidelberg Catechism is the best guidance for our preaching, teaching, and pastoral care.

Nevertheless one rightly feels that the Catechism of Heidelberg has something about it which differs in many points from other expressions of the Reformed faith. This difference is not a question of doctrine but of atmosphere. In the Palatinate the Elector and the church leaders wished to be Reformed but, like their great countryman and adviser, Melanchthon, they disliked the controversies raised in those years by the Lutheran theologians of the second generation, about whom Calvin had written to Bul-

The Catechism in Historical Context

linger: "I have no confidence any longer in those who ape Luther."[17] Calvin, who had sought union with the Lutherans with the utmost exertion, was disillusioned in the last period of his life.

But the Palatine Church, where Melanchthon's spirit was alive, kept the door open for unity. From the letter of Olevianus to Calvin we can conclude that the name of Calvin was not more acceptable than that of other Reformers. Frederick III was proud that he had not read one letter of Zwingli or of Calvin. He and his theologians desired to be biblical, and as biblical, also irenic and ecumenical. In that warm biblical spirit the Catechism was written.

There is yet another reason for its original mark. The Catechism is a unity of the Reformed mind and the German tongue. The Reformed mind loves sharp ideas and clear definitions. The same can be said about the mind of Melanchthon which also contributed so much to the Catechism. The German language is less sharp than the Latin and the French but it has more depth and warmth. This combination of mind and language, carried out by irenical theologians had a result that is unique. Everyone who has had the privilege of preaching or of teaching the Catechism knows how this unity of sharp wording and clear composition with biblical and personal warmth appeals both to the heart and to the intellect of those who hear and read it. And whoever has had the doubtful privilege of cooperating in an effort to create a new book for confessional and catechetical use has experienced the well-nigh impossible task of imitating this wonderful synthesis.

AN ECUMENICAL GUIDE

For all these reasons we possess in the Heidelberg Catechism a preeminently biblical and ecumenical guide for our Christian faith. Philip Schaff characterized it in this way: "Here the mind of Melanchthon and the mind of Calvin joined hands and the Heidelberg Catechism bears the clear marks of both. It unites Melanchthonian mildness and fervor with Calvinian power and depth."[18] George W. Richards says: "One may define it as Calvinism modified by the German genius."[19] And Lang writes:

> By all this the Heidelberg Catechism within Reformed Protestantism has received, so to say, an ecumenical character. A broad bridge leads from it to the Lutheran sister-confession. Within its own church again and again different theologies (e.g., those of Voetius and Cocceius) and various religious trends (e.g., Orthodoxy and Pietism) were able to build on it. This ecumenical character—and that is in my opinion its specific theological characteristic—is based on the fact that the Heidelberg Catechism . . . has understood how to summarize the most effective religious and ethical basic motifs of Reformed Protestantism and how to render them almost constantly in a simple biblical purity.[20]

It has done its uniting work down the centuries; first in Germany, afterward also in the United States. The foreword of the new American edition published by the United Church Press says:

> We are hopeful that this summary of evangelical teaching may, in our time, become a unitive confession not only for Lutheran and Reformed theologians, as it already was in the sixteenth century, but also for Congregational Christian and Evangelical and Reformed people in the United Church of Christ, for Presbyterian and Reformed Churches within the Alliance, and for an even wider fellowship of churches committed to the twentieth-century venture of reuniting the church, catholic, reformed, and evangelical.

CHAPTER FIVE

The Catechism as an Expression of Our Faith

IN CONSIDERING THE CONTENT of the Catechism and its actual relevance, it is necessary to be selective and to indicate only a few points of interpretation that are of exceptional or little known riches and to show the significance of certain passages for our faith and confession today.

QUESTION 1

One wonders whether this long sentence (Question 1) with its many subsentences is a good beginning for a catechism which is to be taught to children. But no one can doubt that here we have a climax of the confessional literature of all Christian ages. It is a fine example of the synthesis of personal warmth and intellectual clarity. It shows a well-considered composition. Beginning with Christ who has saved me, it continues with the Father who protects me and ends with the Holy Spirit who assures me of eternal life and conditions my will. Parallel to this Trinitarian composition is the division into past, present, and future: I have been freed; I am now protected; I expect eternal life.

After this description of the gospel, the last words remind us of the Law: the Holy Spirit "makes me wholeheartedly willing and ready from now on to live for him." No word is superfluous. Christ saves us not only from the guilt but also from the power of sin. He does his work for us, and also in us. We are his possession, but that means deliverance and his other gifts of grace.

Even more important is the existential approach to the content of faith. No plurality of creedal objects is displayed. No abstract God, no objectivistic truth is the starting point of Christian discipleship. But neither is this point to be sought in an abstract man, in subjectivistic religion, or in a presupposed conception of existence. The starting point is the union of a real God and a real man in an encounter which is real and relevant because it is an encounter of dissimilar persons. It is my comfort that I belong to my faithful Savior, Jesus Christ.

The Reformation has cut off the dialectical method of Scholasticism and replaced it (alas, but for a short time) with what Thomas F. Torrance calls "dialogical theology." Faith, confession, and theology do not arise from an abstract intellectual contemplation of God and man, but from the situation of an encounter in which the Word of God comes to us and summons us to answer and to surrender. Nevertheless, most of the confessions and catechisms do not have their starting point in the encounter itself. And none other does it in such a radical way as our first question does. Here we have the synthesis between a more Lutheran approach which asks how I may get to know a gracious God, and a more Reformed approach which asks how we may glorify God.

This method is even more relevant today than it was four centuries ago. The seventeenth century was objectivistic; the nineteenth century, subjectivistic. The twentieth century tries to overcome this unprofitable antithesis. But Rudolf Bultmann who takes his position in a philosophical preconception of existence and who considers the cross of Christ as the means to confirm our existence, gets himself mixed in subjectivism, with unfortunate consequences for preaching and teaching. At the same time we cannot regress to objectivism. The legitimate reaction against it by Friedrich Schleiermacher and his successors might have led to an approach which was neither theocentric nor anthropocentric but pneumatocentric. In his famous study on Schleiermacher, Karl Barth has said that Schleiermacher meant, but failed, to project such a theology.

Our Question 1 offers the starting point for it. It is little won-

The Catechism as an Expression of Our Faith

der that Heinrich Ott, who has been influenced by Bultmann, but tries to avoid his existentialistic subjectivism, has gladly welcomed Question 1 as pointing out the right way and has written a book on the first Sundays of the Heidelberg Catechism as a model for a sound theological approach. This reminds us that Question 1 is not yet behind us but calling us for further treatment.

The Catechism's existential approach does not lead to an impoverishment of the faith, but to a full catholic and Trinitarian display of it. Moreover the Trinitarian approach does not stand here, as in many recent discussions, over against a Christological one, but is, on the contrary, the unfolding of it. We belong to Jesus Christ. His protection is the protection of his Father, and his assurance of eternal life. His guidance in ethical decisions is carried out by him through his Holy Spirit. Further, the whole of this Christocentric-trinitarian work is not a remote and strange work, but the fulfillment of our deepest personal needs: it is "our only comfort in life and in death."

The word comfort is often misunderstood. It sounds like a mood of the individual soul—as does its opposite, wretchedness or misery. But the second question makes clear that misery means far more than this and that it points to an objective situation. In our time we would use the word estrangement. So comfort is something like shelter. In those ages with their many wars, epidemics, disasters of nature, high mortality, and fear of eternal judgment, the words *miseria* and *consolatio* had far more connotations than we now hear in them. They did not express an egotistic sentimental piety, but the deepest existential concerns of life. The Catechism, with admirable precision, exactly chose those words which could help people to recognize the relevance of the gospel. We need not repeat their words, but we must do with our words today what they did with theirs for their time.

This wonderful, radical, catholic, serious yet happy, confession should be learned by heart by everyone who wishes to become a communicant member of a Reformed church. As a former minister, as well as personally, I know what it means to people to be accompanied by these words during life's pilgrimage. I have known many for whom they were an anchor on their deathbed.

QUESTION 2

Though the word comfort dominates the first question, it does not control the entire Catechism. That is left to three other words: wretchedness, redemption, gratitude. Take one of these away and you take them all away. They form a unity which is expressed in the first question. Without them we cannot live and die in the blessedness of this comfort.

So they are meant to be a display of the content of the word comfort. This is not always well understood. The right-wing Pietism in the Netherlands, e.g., considers the three words as pointing to three stages of spiritual experience through which one has to pass successively. So, first the Law has to bring us to despair, then the awareness of redemption is worked by the Holy Spirit, and finally, if there is time left in this earthly life, the converted one comes to the stage of gratitude. In these groups the Catechism is loved and preached as the chronological description of regenerated life.

But on many points the Catechism resists this manner of reading; it does not think in stages. The three words do not point to a chronological but to a logical order. They are preceded by the only comfort and they display its essential elements. If we come to faith in Jesus Christ, in principle we receive all three in one. There is no knowledge of grace without gratitude and without knowledge of sin. All three are given in Christ although psychologically different aspects of this one composite truth can dominate in the life of a Christian at different times.

The wording of Question 2 has often raised criticism: "How many things must you know?" After the existential approach of the first question this sounds like a backsliding into objectivism. But an existential approach is different from an existentialistic one. "Existentialistic" stands over against "objectivistic." But biblical existentiality, describing the encounter of dissimilar persons, presupposes a divine objectivity which is discovered and confessed in the existential encounter. God's deeds are one and many at the same time; we have to know many things in order to understand the only comfort. In its seemingly naïve words the Catechism is ahead of our short-lived, twentieth-century controversies.

The Catechism as an Expression of Our Faith
QUESTIONS 3-11

The division concerning wretchedness is by far the shortest one. It includes nine out of 129 questions. Its brevity shows that the Reformation, though deeply impressed by our guilt and condemnation, is not a "pessimistic" type of faith and has no independent interest in the doctrine of sin. We have to know the depth of our sin in order to know the height of God's grace.

It is remarkable that in this catechism, the summary of the Law as Jesus gave it in the "great commandment" is presented as the source of our knowledge of sin and not, as is usual, the Decalog itself (Question 4). So at the very beginning of our knowledge of sin there is mention of the name of him who in the first question was introduced as our Savior and Protector. His law says: you shall love the Lord your God and your neighbor. And this love is shown nowhere in the Scriptures as a spontaneous act of our own initiative, but an answer, a reflection, a reaction of the love of God in Christ toward us: "We love because he first loved us."

The Reformation, particularly in its Lutheran shape, is in danger of putting the Law as an independent entity over against the gospel, and to misjudge the basic unity of revelation. This danger is here cut off. The Law is embedded in the gospel. This is in accordance with the findings of biblical theology in our time. Sin, in the biblical sense of the word, is not transgression of separate commandments, of natural law, or of general standards. It is a personal act, the distortion of our personal relation with God and our neighbor. We sin against love and we do not know what our sin really is without knowing the love of God. Confession of sin and confession of faith belong together. Our Savior is our accuser. That gives to the knowledge of our wretchedness its horrible depth but at the same time its limits.

"By nature I am prone to hate God and my neighbor." This frank statement of the result of the confrontation of man with the law of love has scandalized many. It looks so exaggerated and seems to neglect the many good qualities and achievements of mankind. And do we really hate God and our neighbor? The law of love says that God has to stand uppermost in our judgments and decisions, and that he is immediately followed by our neighbor; we ourselves have to have third place. In our sinful reality this order is basically and continuously reversed. As "love" in its biblical sense does not mean primarily a sentiment but an act of will, a decision in favor of anyone (whom we may like or may not like); so "hate" means not to acknowledge anyone's legitimate place in our decisions and actions, to neglect or misuse him. That is exactly what we daily do with God and our neighbor. The Catechism truly is not too harsh; it is rather too friendly as it says no more than that I am prone to hate!

One must read Questions 5-11 without interruption to discover the power of this mighty indictment. Every answer takes away another reason for excuse. We hear the echo of Israel's prophets who accused the people of having repudiated the covenant-love of God. Nevertheless there is also a danger in these questions, especially in the last ones. In the development of the indictment the knowledge of sin becomes more and more isolated from the knowledge of Christ and his love. God's righteousness and wrath become isolated and abstract qualities. The Catechism does not stick here to its fine initial unity of Law and gospel, of righteousness and mercy. Now they are put asunder: "God is indeed merciful and gracious, but he is also righteous" (Question 11). The consequences of this tendency are found in the next questions.

QUESTIONS 12-19

The questions on the necessity of the incarnation are the least beloved part of the Catechism. The reasoning which is followed gives the impression that the possibility, the necessity, and even the reality of the incarnation can be logically deduced like the answer to a mathematical problem. We know three classical works which try to prove the logic of the incarnation: Athanasius' *The Incarnation of the Word,* Anselm's *Why Did God Become Man?* and the Heidelberg Catechism (Questions 12-19). Athanasius deduces the necessity of incarnation from the combination of veracity and goodness in God; Anselm, from that of justice and mercy, and the Catechism does also. Often this method is characterized as rationalism, i.e., as an excessive confidence in the power of reason to discover the cohesion and even the facts of divine reality. But this is not true either for Athanasius, for Anselm, or for the Catechism. All three have their starting point not in reason but in the data of biblical revelation. How else would we know about God's justice, mercy, and veracity?

The questions which the Catechism puts forward, e.g., "What kind of mediator and redeemer must we seek?" are questions which nobody asks by natural reasoning. Moreover, the answer to these questions, the person of Jesus Christ, is known to us, as Answer 19 states, "from the holy gospel" and from nowhere else. So the method is not rationalistic. But what may then be its meaning? Based on the reality of revelation, the Catechism wants to prove its inner cohesion and the necessity of incarnation from the point of view of the other data of revelation. One can defend this attempt as a legitimate one. We are reminded of the frequent use of the word must in the New Testament. Christ must be rejected; he must die and rise; "he had to be made like his brethren in every respect" (Heb. 2:17); "it was fitting that we should have such a high priest" (Heb. 7:26). Of course these words of the Scriptures are confessions, not reasonings. But why should not theology, in which we desire to love God with our intelligence, go a step further? Anselm said, *"Credo ut intelligam!"* And Barth, his congenial follower, who wrote a book on his method, on several occasions defended the legitimacy of what the Catechism is doing here.[1]

That is right in part. Nevertheless Barth acknowledges that we must not follow this method.[2] It looks too much like building the knowledge of reality on the rational conviction of its necessity. So the problem of the legitimacy of Questions 12-19 returns. We cannot avoid asking the following questions: What can we know about the necessity of the fact and the way of our salvation beyond its facticity? Are there any motives for God's mercy other than mercy itself? If we could know other reasons, would we not misjudge God's freedom? And above all: would we not take away the element of surprise and therefore violate the mystery of free grace? Moreover, in speaking about God's mercy in conflict and combination with his righteousness, are we not in danger of violating the unity of God and of ascribing to him a kind of schizophrenia?

For all these reasons we cannot endorse the method of this

part of the Catechism. It transgresses the limits of revelation and faith and leads into the fields of abstraction and speculation. Questions like these are artificial; nobody can ask them except he already know the answers and no longer need ask them! We understand the purpose of the Catechism: to convince its readers that nothing short of the incarnation was necessary to rescue us. But the divine fact itself is convincing enough; every piece of human reasoning obscures the power of its facticity. We are happy that this method is an exception in the Catechism and that from here on without interruption it continues to instruct us in the spirit of the first question.

QUESTION 21

This is a new height: here in Question 21 is proffered the famous definition of faith. Some people are of a different opinion, considering the wording "not only a certain knowledge . . . but also a wholehearted trust," as—so to speak—a way of putting asunder what God has joined together. They remind us of the fact that Ursinus was a follower of Melanchthon and that this twofold definition stems from Melanchthon's somewhat scholastic separation of elements which in reality form a unity. Moreover Ursinus' later works, they say, show that this separation seduced him into putting the element of knowledge, as merely historical, outside of redemptive faith, which devaluation of the element of knowledge opened the way to sentimental and introspective Pietism. They notice also that according to Question 21, trust is created by the Holy Spirit, but that nothing similar is said of knowledge.

We do injury to the Catechism as well as to Melanchthon, however, if we judge them by a later misuse of their twofold definition. (Ursinus himself became more scholastic in his later years.) The words "knowledge" and "trust" are not related as a lower and a higher grade, nor is their order meant to indicate succession. Questions 1 and 2 have the order reversed; the two words do not describe two realities but one reality under two aspects. By putting the two words in one phrase the Catechism enjoins that the demand for truth and the demand for salvation find one and the same divine answer.

The Catechism as an Expression of Our Faith

In the Middle Ages the church was accustomed to expressing the meaning of the word faith in only one word: knowledge (*notitia*) or agreement (*assensus*). So faith lost its biblical depth and degenerated into a merely intellectual act which had to be completed by love. By using two words to describe one reality, the Reformation gave back to the conception of faith its true biblical fullness. In many cases theology needs to speak in two words in order to maintain the depth and height of God's revelation: Christ, true God and true man; gospel and Law; justification and sanctification; the church as institute and community. The risk is ever present that people who do not understand what is really meant will treat the two words as expressing two different realities. But in their togetherness they describe one reality. The word trust does not add a new element to that of "knowledge" but expresses the personal dimension and tendency of the biblical knowledge. The Reformers could not do without these two words—and neither can we.

This fact becomes even clearer if we do not stick to these two words as such, but read them in their context: "It is not only a certain knowledge by which I accept as true all that God has revealed to us in his Word, but also a wholehearted trust . . . that, not only to others, but to me also God has given the forgiveness of sins." The Catechism says that there is no real knowledge of revelation if you have not discovered the personal tendency of that revelation. All that is revealed has been revealed to comfort you. In the Middle Ages there were good reasons to warn against an isolation of knowledge, and an ecclesiastical collectivism in which one does not come to the point of personal acceptance and surrender. That warning holds good today.

But to us this twofold definition is also relevant for the opposite reason. Men like Albrecht Ritschl and Rudolf Bultmann and their followers have defined faith one-sidedly as confidence and have considered the element of knowledge as alien to the true faith. As the Reformation has to say to the Middle Ages: your so-called knowledge is not the biblical knowledge; so it has to say to these recent theologies: your so-called trust is not the biblical trust. Confidence in God always means confidence in his concrete words and deeds—in the plural. Only in the knowledge of this plural do we find the singular of personal encounter and comfort. Indeed, the twofold definition of Question 21 is today as relevant as it was four hundred years ago.

QUESTION 22

The next question confirms our explanation of Question 21. It is a repetition of the same motives. "What must a Christian believe?"—thus the question of knowledge is posed. The answer is: "All that is promised us in the gospel, a summary of which is taught us in the articles of the Apostles' Creed." Every article is a historical fact. And these facts are as such promises. That is the reason why the Catechism in explaining the articles so often asks: "What benefit do you receive from?" or a similar phrase. I know no classic of the Reformation in which the acts of divine revelation on the one hand and their existential relevance on the other hand are kept together so well and so consistently. Here is the true medicine against Roman Catholicism and Existentialism, against intellectual Orthodoxy and sentimental Pietism or Liberalism.

QUESTION 26

Question 26 opens the explanation of the articles of the Creed. For many centuries, almost from the very beginning of Christian theology, the doctrines of creation and providence were considered as "mixed articles," i.e., as truths about which one could have also some knowledge apart from the Christian revelation. The consequence was that these doctrines were treated without regard to the revelation in Jesus Christ and personal faith, as a kind of philosophy in which one can have insight by reason and experience only.

The Reformation broke with this tradition. We know the famous words of Luther's Small Catechism: "I believe that God has created me together with all creatures, and still preserves me." Here the first article is a personal confession and no longer philosophical reasoning. In the Catechism of Geneva Calvin links creation and providence with the revelation in Jesus Christ. Question 22 reads: "Why do you call him Father? It is with reference to Christ who is his eternal Word." At the close of the

The Catechism as an Expression of Our Faith

answer the personal element is found also: "But since God is the Father of Jesus Christ, it follows that he is our Father also."

The Catechism of Heidelberg stands in the same tradition, but surpasses all similar pronouncements in strength. Not only is the word Father explained as being connected with the word Son in the second article, but the Catechism says that this God is "for the sake of Christ his Son, my God and my Father" and that therefore I trust in him completely, in his governing of the world and of my personal fate. So we have no access to the confession of creation and providence except through the confession of re-creation and salvation. Without Christ, as Calvin said, the world is a labyrinth in which we get lost. We first believe in Christ and for his sake in providence, not the other way around.

This way of setting forth God's governance of the world is a real liberation which we feel even more in modern times. We suffer more than former generations from the untransparency of the world and from what we call the absence of God. The world looks like an absurd mixture of fate and accident, of guilt and high tragedy. This experience alienates us from much Christian piety, theology, and philosophy. But it brings us nearer to the Bible, e.g., to the book of Job and to the words: "By faith we understand that the world was created by the word of God" (Heb. 11:3). Only in the personal encounter with Jesus Christ as the evidence of God's mighty love toward us, do we dare to believe that the same love is the deepest secret of our and the whole world's life and fate.

Old Testament scholars like Jacob, von Rad, Vriezen, and others have made clear that, although the Old Testament begins with creation, the faith of Israel originally was the faith in God's saving acts for his people, in the exodus, the protection in the desert, the entry into the promised land, the victory over their enemies. These deeds were the evidence that Jahweh was mightier than all other gods, and this conviction led to the confession that Jahweh was the Creator and Lord of the whole world. In accordance with these biblical insights Barth, in his doctrine of creation and providence, follows the same path from salvation in Christ to the confession of creation and preservation. No wonder that Question 26 is much beloved and frequently quoted by him.

No confession is nearer to our present insights into the relation between the confession of God the Redeemer and the confession of God the Creator than this question of the Catechism.

QUESTION 27

The next question, as it describes the way and the realms of divine providence, suddenly seems to have lost the Christological perspective of the former question. In addition, the numbering of the phenomena in which God's providence works has raised much criticism in our time. It looks as if the welfare of the individual faithful Christian is the ultimate aim of God's preservation of the world. But this remark may be unfair. We have to do with a confession of personal faith and as such it is an interpretation of many words of the Scriptures, e.g., Romans 8:28.

Another objection is that although rain and drought come to us by his fatherly hand, this cannot be said in the same way about riches and poverty. Here we feel the danger of a kind of belief in providence which can create social quietism and make the church indulgent in injustice and social inequities. Our generation with its tremendous accomplishments in science and techniques knows what the Catechism did not know: to what extent man can change the world and play an important role in the shaping of providence. We would now have to phrase this question in other words; we would have to say also that it belongs to God's providence that he has appointed man to control and develop his creation, and that in our human achievements we may see a great sign of the divine providence. But at the same time we know that every achievement creates new problems and threats and that our dependence grows with our independency.

Looking to our crucified and risen Lord, we may confess concerning the totality of our ambiguous situation that it comes to us by God's fatherly hand and that in everything he works for good with those who love him. So we are back at the essential content of Question 27 and can agree with the beautiful words in which Question 28 describes what it calls the advantage of this confession.

The Catechism as an Expression of Our Faith

QUESTION 32

Christological questions follow. It strikes one that their order is interrupted by Question 32. After having asked: "Why is he called Christ," the Catechism goes on: "But why are you called a Christian?" This is not only another evidence of the practical existential tendency of this entire manual of instruction; it also proves that the Catechism emphasizes the work of Christ in us as well as his work for us. The Reformation was not reactionary. Its focus was on justification by faith, but it did not forget for one moment the significance of sanctification. We are not only the objects of justification; Christ makes us also to be subjects with him—to be prophets, priests, and kings with him. This is what Paul calls our becoming conformed to the image of the Son and what Question 86 calls our becoming renewed according to his image.

Here I see a trend which we miss in much European preaching and teaching—to our disadvantage. Orthodoxy speaks about Christ as our Savior; Liberalism speaks about Christ as our example; the Catechism speaks about him who in his very work as our Savior becomes our example.

QUESTION 34

"Why do you call him our lord?" The answer to Question 34 surprises us. There is no word about obedience and responsibility. The title *kurios* is interpreted purely as an expression of comfort, of our being bought and sheltered.

QUESTION 44

In impressive words Question 44 gives Calvin's explanation of the descent into hell. The order of the Creed proves that this interpretation cannot be the true historical one. We have to think of an event between burial and resurrection, i.e., a dwelling of Christ in the realm of the dead. The Reformed interpretation is a remarkable specimen of existential demythologizing of the oldest tradition. At the Synod of Dort (1618-1619) the Catechism was also subject to discussion. All approved of it, but the representatives of the reformed church of England (now the Anglican

Church) expressed their disagreement with the interpretation of the descent into hell. The Synod took note of this deviation from the Catechism but did not consider it as a difference in doctrine.

QUESTION 45

Question 45 is a good example of the synthesis of clear composition and warm devotion. The personal benefit of Christ's resurrection is described in three sentences, which in excellent brevity sum up three of its aspects: resurrection for us, in us, and in the future. The emphasis is Christological, pneumatological, and eschatological.

QUESTIONS 47 AND 48

Now we have to look at two questions (47-48) which have been heavily discussed and attacked in these four centuries. The first attack was delivered as early as May 4, 1563 in the *Anweisung* of the Lutheran theologians Brenz and Andreae. Since that time these questions have remained a stumbling block to the Lutherans; and they have also increasingly become an embarrassment to the Reformed theology.

There is something mysterious in these polemical questions in the midst of this irenic and ecumenical booklet. What can have urged the authors to put them in? A possible reason is that Tilemann Hesshus strongly emphasized the ubiquity of Christ's human nature as the ground of his real presence at the Holy Table; and that the influence of his short but fanatical activity was still felt in the Palatinate. In that case we can understand that a refutation was deemed necessary. But even then we must ask why the church should confuse the minds of children and common people with such scholastic distinctions as are made here.

Question 47 puts asunder what in the act of incarnation belongs inseparately together. Is the Christ who promises to us: "I am with you always," but a half Christ, only the divine half? To say that Christ as a man is no longer on earth, but that he is never absent in his divinity is hardly less than a heresy which undermines the personal union of the two natures in Christ, a heresy which the Lutherans did not fail to label and to attack as Nestorianism. But their counterdoctrine of the *communicatio idiomatum* and the omnipresence of Christ's human nature was heretical as well because it denied the real humanity of the risen Lord. Reformed thinkers stigmatized it as Eutychianism or Monophysitism.

Question 48, though asking the very thing that is decisive here, nevertheless gives an answer which makes matters even worse. It points out that the Godhead of Christ transcends the bounds of human nature—a statement which as such is true and is even a common Christian heritage (Athanasius, Augustine) and so wrongly known as the *Extra Calvinisticum*. In this context, however, the answer can but strengthen the impression that after the ascension we have to do on this earth with an abstract Godhead only.

If the *Extra Calvinisticum* is not treated as the reverse of the confession of the Godhead "intra" humanity, this theologoumenon is accepted at the cost of Christ's true descent and of the *unio hypostatica*. We understand that Reformed theologians pleaded the cause of God's sublimity and freedom, but paid a high price. The discussion was endless—a sign that both confessions had enough biblical truth to defend themselves but not enough to convince the others. With their deification of humanity, the Lutherans had to maintain and explain Christ's humiliation in his earthly life. To do that they entangled themselves more and more in queer and abstract theories about *krupsis* (concealing) or *kenosis* (emptying) of the divine nature. These theories no longer have defenders; nor is the doctrine of the *communicatio idiomatum* a living element in the Lutheran heritage.

And the Reformed position? The wording of the Catechism does not find much defense either. As Paul Jacobs rightly says: "These languages are no longer spoken today."[3] The pages which G. C. Berkouwer dedicates to these passages in his book *The Work of Christ* are an exception. In Berkouwer's opinion the sole purpose of the Catechism is to exclude a bodily presence of the Lord since his ascension, in accordance with the words in the Scriptures that speak of Christ as being no longer on earth (Matthew 26:11; John 16:28; 17:11; Acts 3:21; Hebrews 8:4). He even asserts that the Catechism only wishes to indicate the nature of Christ's presence.

It may be that this is the deepest and the pure purpose lying behind the phraseology. But we have to do with the concrete words which not only exclude the bodily presence of Christ, but the presence of his human nature in general.[4] So I cannot avoid agreeing with Barth who characterizes these questions as "an accident of theological labor" and who writes: "Through these two questions we learn how dangerous it is for a partner in a theological discussion to be seduced by a false thesis so that he puts forward a false counterthesis."[5] What he means by that he explains in his *Kirchliche Dogmatik* in the paragraph about God's omnipresence, where he distinguishes between different modes and grades of God's presence in creating reality. He writes:

> Together with the Reformed we must distinguish and say: Christ is there (i.e., in heaven) essentially and originally present and here symbolically, sacramentally, spiritually. But with the Lutherans we must take these together and say: he is not less here than there; he is there and here really present, there and here the total Christ in his divine and in his human nature.[6]

Another way in which we might seek to come together (but basically the same way) is, as I see it, in a deeper study of the relation of the Spirit to Christ. The Spirit is nothing other than the active presence of the ascended Christ, different from his bodily presence, but none the less the real presence of the total Christ in accordance with his glorified status, though less than the mode of presence which we believe to take place in the great future. All of this means that our generation, more biblical than speculative as we are, is less certain than our ancestors, not about Christ's presence among us, but about the validity of the human formulations in which we describe it. We are less inclined to fight with others about their inadequate verbal expressions than to seek with others more adequate expressions.

QUESTION 52

Next we turn to the question (52) about the last judgment. The admirable answer puts an end to an agelong tradition in which this article of the Creed was treated as a reason for nothing but anxiety and dismay. We think of the hymn *Dies Irae* of Thomas of Celano, of the medieval penitential sermons, of Michelangelo's painting in the Sistine Chapel in Rome. The Christ that they present to us is not the suffering servant, the redeemer of the sinners, but the condemning conqueror who fulminates against sinners. In the medieval mind there were almost two Christs, the Christ of redemption and the Christ of judgment.

The answer of the Catechism has restored the biblical unity of gospel and Law. "To judge" is the translation of the Greek *krinein* which, in its turn, is the translation of the Hebrew *shafat*, meaning as does the German word *richten* "to make right, to restore the right shape of the world by humiliating the proud and elevating the oppressed." The coming of the Judge is part of the gospel! In consequence of what is said in Answer 22 the Catechism holds this article as an element of "all that is promised us in the gospel." We can now confine ourselves to quoting the beautiful key words in the original: *"Dass ich . . . eben des Richters der sich zuvor dem Gerichte Gottes für mich dargestellt, und alle Vermaledeiung von mir hinweg genommen hat, auss dem Himmel gewertig bin."*

QUESTION 54

Question 54 is one of the best known. It is an impressive example of the gift of the authors to express a world of thought in one short sentence. Christ's attitude toward his church is described in three verbs: gather, protect, preserve. The means of this threefold action is indicated in the words "by his Spirit and his Word." The time of this action is "from the beginning to the end of the world." The extent is "the whole human race." The result of this action is not called "church" as in the question itself, but *Gemein* (congregation).

Nothing is said here about institution, order, or ministry; a church is a community with the Lord and with one another. And this community is *auserwelte Gemein*—elected, chosen for eternal life. Predestination is mentioned only here and then only in its positive side of election. Moreover, election is related to a community and only through it to the individual who is introduced in the last sentence which eloquently expresses the certainty of faith. So the emphasis on the connection of election and community does not mean collectivism, but points out that we find our certainty only if we seek the Spirit in the realm of Word and sacrament, in the community of believers.

We deplore the fact that Reformed theology later on did not keep in mind this biblical order and tendency, but instead developed a more and more individualistic conception of predestination. The result was that it fostered introspection and so lost the certainty of faith, the central reality in which Luther had the advantage over the Roman Catholic Church.

QUESTION 55

Question 55 corresponds exactly with the ambiguities of the Latin expression *communio sanctorum* which can have three meanings: communion with the saints (in heaven), communion with the sacred things, or the communion of saints with one another. The answer puts the first and the second meaning together in the words: "as partakers of the Lord Christ and all his treasures and gifts." The one saint, Jesus Christ, here replaces the many saints of tradition.

QUESTION 58

The explanation of the Creed is concluded in Question 58. It does not advocate a mere futuristic eschatology as many sects do. Nor does it interpret eschatology as an expression for the eternal value of the encounter with Christ here and now, as is in fashion today in certain German theological schools. Nor does it consider eternal life as a compensation and projection of human lack and desire. It conceives the future as a display of what we now possess already in principle. Thus it has the same approach as biblical theology. But this recent movement finds the "now" mostly in Christology, whereas the Catechism seeks it in the reality of the Spirit.

This is a good, biblical, and necessary approach: The Spirit is the firstfruit, the guarantee, the "down payment" of the eternal future. Here the Catechism has to correct and to complement us.

The Catechism as an Expression of Our Faith

Taste these abundant words: "Since I now feel . . . the beginning of eternal joy!" The word joy is used more than once in the Catechism (see also Question 90, which speaks of "complete joy in God"). It shows that the key word comfort does not point to a minimum wrung from desperation but to a maximum granted by the Spirit.

QUESTIONS 59-64

We come now to what for the Reformers was the heart of the matter: justification by faith and the relation of faith and works (Questions 59-64). The core of the Reformed faith is expressed in Question 60. The answer is too long from a didactical point of view, but what a careful and powerful phraseology!

The expression "justification by faith" is an unhappy and incorrect one. It is not our faith which justifies us, but the sole reconciling work of Jesus Christ. Faith is a mere instrument by which we receive what Christ has achieved for us. Faith is, as Matthias Flacius said, the begging hand (*manus mendica*).

The threat of a misunderstanding of faith as the ground of our righteousness is taken away by the clear answer of Question 61. The Reformers were highly alert on this point. It is nevertheless a lasting feature of Reformed spirituality that many of its followers are inclined to believe in their own belief. They seek in themselves the evidence of a living faith. But nobody can objectify his own faith. Faith is not a thing, but an act, entirely directed toward and exclusively interested in its object: the grace of God in Jesus Christ. To believe means no longer to believe in one's self, in one's own convictions and sentiments, in one's religion and piety, but in him who alone is our righteousness before God. If our preaching and pastoral ministry would stick to this severe yet mild, deep, and broad truth of the justification of the ungodly, what deliverance that would bring to the self-centered and introspective, and therefore so uncertain, minds of our fellow Christians!

The next questions deal with works. We admire the wonderful balance of thought which at the same time is the right pastoral guide. Christ received by faith, is our sole redemption. Nothing which comes from ourselves can contribute to our justification.

The radical nature of this message, which is both humiliating and liberating, preserves the Christian joy in us. But that does not mean that nothing happens in us. Faith alone justifies, but faith never remains alone. All that has to be said here Question 64 expresses in the well-chosen and well-known words: "It is impossible for those who are ingrafted into Christ by true faith not to bring forth the fruit of gratitude." These words do not take away anything of the Christian's deliverance and the joy, but they do prevent us from thinking of grace as something which remains outside of us and which does not work in us.

QUESTIONS 65-85

A remarkably large part of the Catechism is taken up by the exposition of the sacraments with an appendix on the keys of heaven—the latter being merely a prolongation of the doctrine of the Holy Supper. The fact that no less than twenty-one questions (65-85) are dedicated to the sacraments is one of the many evidences that the Reformation was far from negative. The very sacraments, which had been so badly mistreated in the medieval church, received much attention and were not removed or neglected in favor of the preaching of the Word. The Reformers did not wish to be the cause of a reaction or a revolution, but just what the name says—a reformation, also of the doctrine and practice of the sacraments.

In the Heidelberg Catechism this careful attention given the nature of the sacraments even goes so far as to neglect the doctrine of the Word and preaching. And this is in spite of the fact that the, so to speak, sacramental character of the preached Word as the consubstantiation of the divine Word in, with, and under the human words is one of the great discoveries and renewals of the Reformation. But here, where we expect an exposition of it, it seems to be absent. That is not quite true however. We find a deep expression of the significance and working of the preached Word in Question 84, where the sermon is presented as one of the two keys by which the kingdom of heaven is opened to believers and shut against unbelievers. Apart from the question whether this explanation of the keys expresses the meaning of

The Catechism as an Expression of Our Faith

Matthew 16:19, we have here an unsurpassed description of the divine authority of preaching.

Now we turn to the sacraments. The Catechism displays the typical Calvinistic doctrine which we can identify by the use of parallelism: "as certainly as" we partake in an earthly, visible action, "so" we communicate in a spiritual reality. These two realities are separate, but connected by the promise of God and the action of the Holy Spirit. This parallelism, a heritage of Augustine which we can find in Questions 69, 73, 75, 77, 78, and 79, excludes on the left hand Zwinglian symbolism and on the right hand Lutheran and Roman realism.

The doctrine has found a peculiar consequence in its application to the Holy Supper. Calvin understood the words of institution "this is my body . . . this is my blood" as pointing to the human and even bodily aspect of Christ. At the same time he believed, as we have said, that Christ's humanity is no longer with us, but in heaven. So he taught that as certainly as we eat and drink at the table we communicate through the Holy Spirit by the mouth of faith with Christ's body and blood in heaven. This strange construction has its echo in Question 76.

We perceive the function of this theologoumenon in that period. By it Calvin maintained the divine reality of the sacraments against Zwinglianism and at the same time avoided what in his eyes was a fleshly or even idolatrous realism. The price however is a theological construction that does not appeal to our faith and has no real relation with the symbolical event at the Holy Table. This theory had its value in a time when the real presence was considered as being exclusively connected with the elements of bread and wine and when it seemed that there was no other alternative to symbolism and realism.

In the last decades many New Testament scholars, especially in Germany, have given much energy to clarify the meaning of Jesus' words in the upper room. We now know that "body and blood" is the expression for the total person, that the real presence is related to the action of eating and drinking as a whole, and that the Holy Supper is the fulfillment of the meals with disciples, sinners, and publicans. Moreover, it is itself fulfilled in the meals after the resurrection and is finally—or, first of all—the prophetic image and the anticipating enactment of the great wedding feast of the future. All these elements wait for a new Calvin who can create a new synthesis in avoiding the common traditional derailments.

Question 80 is a subject of discussion down to the present. We cannot go into it here, but can only point out what the problem is. Can we still say that the Mass is one of the main points of contradiction with the Roman Catholic Church? Is it really "a complete denial of the once-for-all sacrifice and passion of Jesus Christ and as such an idolatry to be condemned"? The answer depends on how we estimate the recent Eucharistic theories propounded in the Roman Catholic Church and the corresponding reinterpretation of the Tridentine expressions.

In many countries in Europe this "new theology" deeply influences the practice of the celebration of the Eucharist. Some Roman Catholic theologians even characterize the discussion with Luther's consubstantiation as a misunderstanding. But up to the present these new ideas are limited to certain areas and have no official authority. As long as the theories and practices in the Roman Catholic Church are so varied, we had better abstain from pronouncements about the relevance of Answer 80 for the present-day situation.

QUESTION 86

The third division opens with Question 86 which leads from redemption to gratitude. This is another of the many examples of the Catechism's ability to combine brevity and clarity. "Why must we do good works?" The basic answer already has been given in Question 64: "For it is impossible . . . not to bring forth the fruit of gratitude." This "impossible" is now described as resting in the Christ in us, in the renewal through his Spirit according to his own image.

We cannot say that justification is God's work and sanctification, our own. The same Christ who redeems us also renews us, and he makes us active in both: in justification by faith and in sanctification by love. Now this renewal is not so much realized in new inner qualities (as later centuries preferred to present it) as it is in new relations (more in accordance with recent psychologies!),

The Catechism as an Expression of Our Faith

i.e., a renewed relation to God, to ourselves, and to our neighbor. The first and third relation recommend themselves to us at first sight, but the same cannot be said of the wording of the second relation: "that we ourselves may be assured of our faith by its fruits."

Once a person who loved the Catechism very much and really lived in it avowed to me that this was the only passage which he could not understand and accept. This man was and is not alone; these words have given much difficulty. After having read the strong statements in Questions 62 and 63 that even our best works are defiled with sin and have no merit in themselves, one is puzzled to read that our works can assure us of the reality of our faith. This seems to be inconsistent with the Reformed doctrine as a whole. But the Reformers knew nothing of their "doctrine as a whole." They only tried to be—according to the felicitous expression of the Netherlands Confession—"apprentices of Christ"; and some of them were convinced that this "inconsistency" in their "system" was according to scripture.

The doctrine which is presented in these few words is called in the cryptic language of the theologians: *syllogismus practicus,* which means "a syllogism, a sound argument based on the deeds of our practical life." It is a horrible and confusing expression because the spiritual reality to which it points has nothing to do with logical conclusions. From a logical viewpoint these words are even nonsensical. How do we know that our so-called fruits are really fruits of faith? We can know this only if we stand in faith. But in that case we have to do with a sheer circular argument. Moreover, it has dangerous pastoral consequences: it leads people back into the house of bondage of introspection. So it is understandable that again and again criticism is raised concerning these words.

Nevertheless there is a certain trend of thought in the New Testament which makes us hesitate. We think mainly of the first letter of John, where we find such words as: "By this we may be sure that we know him, if we keep his commandments" (2:3); "We know that we have passed out of death into life, because we love the brethren" (3:14); "By this we know that he abides in us, by the Spirit which he has given us" (3:24). Calvin has devoted some clear and careful paragraphs in his *Institutes* to this question (3: 14:18-20). He strongly denies that we can rest on our works for the certainty of our salvation; but, as he says, the works are "complements," "testimonies," which form an a posteriori comfort for the faithful. The works are "as it were, rays of the divine face, . . . testimonies of God's dwelling and governing in us."

Here we have to do with a deep truth indeed. Sometimes the believer is so liberated from the resistance of his flesh that to his own surprise he is urged to do and to say things which are according to God's will but which he never would do by himself. Such fruits are never a reason for pride, but always for humble gratitude. They are encouraging signs that God has not passed over us with his grace.

According to the famous theory of Max Weber this emphasis on the fruits of faith and especially on industrial effort in daily business has stimulated the rise of capitalism, particularly in Great Britain and the United States. If there is such a connection, it is, however, not more than an indirect one.

In the seventeenth century the attention shifted from the *syllogismus practicus* to the *syllogismus mysticus*. Then people did not want to be confirmed in faith by their works but by their inner experience. The classical formulation is given by the Canons of Dort in 1619 where one reads: "The elect become assured of their eternal and irrevocable election . . . when they in themselves observe with a spiritual joy and holy delight the infallible fruits of election indicated in the Word of God, i.e., true faith in Christ, childlike fear of God, godly grief about sin, hunger and thirst for righteousness, and so on" (I, 12). These movements of inner life, however, unlike the outward deeds, are not mentioned in scripture as evidences of faith. The *syllogismus mysticus* of Dort has ushered in a bad period of pietistic introversion. Bible and history together admonish us not to say less or more concerning the signs of grace than Answer 86 does.

QUESTIONS 88-90

Questions 88-90 indicate how the life of gratitude is achieved and maintained. It is by a twofold reality: "the dying of the old self and the birth of the new." This theme of *mortificatio* and *vivificatio* in Christian life is a much-beloved theme of Calvin (see *Institutes,* 3:3:3, 8). It was first touched in a Christological context in Question 43, where we read that "our old self is crucified, put to death, and buried with him"; and in Question 45 which, in connection with the resurrection says: "We too are now raised by his power to a new life." These Christological questions speak about a reality into which we are taken once for all by the dying and rising of Christ, for he is our head and representative. Now in Question 88, however, we deal with the pneumatological aspect. This once-for-all reality has now to be rooted against our nature into our nature, into our existence and actions. This is a struggle which never ends in our earthly life.

The cross of Jesus Christ has to penetrate our daily life. At the cross our human existence of egotism, lust, and self-maintenance underwent a complete annihilation; so now we have to take that seriously in making our daily decisions. That is the dying of the old self or, as Jesus calls it, denying oneself and taking up one's cross. The resurrection of Jesus Christ has to penetrate as well into our daily life. "We have been born anew to a living hope through the resurrection of Jesus Christ from the dead" (1 Peter 1:3). This also must be taken seriously in making our daily decisions. That is the birth of the new self in "complete joy" and "a strong desire to live according to the will of God in all good works" (Question 90).

Dying and rising are not successive acts. They belong together as the two sides of a coin. There is good reason to reverse the order and to speak of "rising and dying," because the renewing Spirit of Christ is the power which enables us to die as old selves. We die to the extent of our rising. But it is at the same time the other way around: only through the hard experience of self-denial do we find the new life in Christ. So we rise to the extent of our dying.[7] These deep and simple words of the Catechism have a high pastoral relevance. Barth reproaches Calvin for overestimating the aspect of dying at the cost of the aspect of rising.[8] The same cannot be said of the Catechism. And we often make our preaching and pastoral work ineffective in that we try to offer a rising without dying. The power of rising shows itself in the readiness to die.

HENDRIKUS BERKHOF
QUESTIONS 92-113

The explanation of the Ten Commandments is found in Questions 92-113. Here the authors follow a definite system. They do not limit themselves to the commandments as they stand, but give a threefold extension: a *broadening* of the actions related to the different commandments, a *deepening* by taking into account also the inner attitude behind the acts, and a *translating* of the negative form of the commandment into a positive one. These three features together lead to a fourth one: the commandments are *applied* to the time of the Catechism itself and so are made contemporary. Look, for example, at the treatment of the sixth commandment in Questions 105-107. Question 105 gives a broadening—among many other deeds suicide is forbidden. Question 106 gives the deepening in speaking of the "root of murder, which is envy, hatred, anger, and desire for revenge." Question 107 translates the negative form into a positive statement: "For when God condemns envy, hatred, and anger, he requires us to love our neighbor as ourselves." This trend is not always given in three questions. The seventh and eighth commandments have it in two (one for the negative and one for the positive); the ninth has it in one question—but the composition is always the same.

As a result of this approach the Catechism gives an application of the Law to its own time. The first commandment forbids enchantments and the invocation of saints; the second one, idols and pictures in the churches (two questions deal with this special subject which was particularly current in the Palatinate at that time); the third commandment forbids unnecessary oaths, but allows oaths required by civil authorities or otherwise needed (this is directed against the Anabaptists); the fourth one requires that the ministry of the gospel and Christian education be maintained; the fifth one is extended to all who are set in authority; the sixth is the justification of a police power; the eighth speaks of false weights and measures, deceptive advertising of merchandising, counterfeit money, and exorbitant interest; the ninth commandment forbids me to be a gossip or a slanderer or to condemn anyone lightly without a hearing.

This topical interpretation is at the same time a special strength

The Catechism as an Expression of Our Faith

and to the very same extent a weakness of the Catechism. Customs, temptations, sins, and ethics are in our time partly the same, partly different. Many preachers dislike dealing with Question 101, about swearing oaths in a devout manner.

The Palatinate Liturgy of the Holy Supper has in its part of preparation a similar topical interpretation of the Ten Commandments. An English translation of this liturgy was used in the great communion service in the New Church in Amsterdam on the occasion of the First Assembly of the World Council of Churches. I am told that Reinhold Niebuhr, when asked concerning his opinion of the list of condemned sins, said that he missed the swindlers and stockbrokers! We have to do for our time, of course, what the Catechism did for its own. Joining in its purpose, we have to say additional or different things. Nevertheless, one may wonder whether even the stockbrokers are not condemned in Question 110! Preachers who are used to explaining this part of the Catechism from the pulpit assure us that they can make the ethical teachings of the Catechism relevant without difficulty.

QUESTIONS 114 AND 115

Our relation to the Law of God in general is spoken of in Questions 114 and 115. They are much loved because they speak right to the heart of the faithful of all times and places. Question 114 treads the narrow path between quietism and perfectionism in speaking on the one hand of "a small beginning" and on the other hand of "serious purpose." Question 115 deals with the two functions of the Law in our lives: first, it makes us conscious of our sinfulness (the so-called *usus elenchticus*); second, it stimulates us to seek our renewal in the image of God (the so-called *usus normativus*). The first function we find in Questions 3-11; the second one, in Questions 91-113. It is typically Reformed (over against Lutheran) to give a broader emphasis to this second function: the Law as a standard for a life lived in gratitude.

QUESTIONS 116-127

Questions 116-127 form the concluding division. They deal with the Lord's Prayer. Here also we find much to admire, especially that the explanations of all the petitions are given in the form of petitions themselves, which is an exception in the catechetical tradition. This part of the Catechism, however, is less important than that which precedes it. The subjects which are treated in the Lord's Prayer are also to be found in the Creed or in the Law in one way or another. So Questions 120 and 121 are an echo of Questions 26-28; Questions 122-124 repeat much of what has been said about Christian obedience; Question 125 reminds us of Question 27; and Question 126, of Questions 56 and 60; Question 127, of Question 114. Moreover the exegesis of the first petitions is debatable; they are interpreted mainly in terms of our responsibility for the kingdom here and now.

An emphasis which is very important, however, is found in the three introductory questions which give directions in general for our prayer life. The sober tone of these directions is striking. Prayer is not seen here as a pouring out of our inner religious emotions, but as "the chief part of the gratitude which God requires of us" (Question 116). Humility and confidence are the twofold conditions of such prayer (Question 117).

QUESTION 129

The closing question is an unexpected and eloquent climax, too little noticed even by the "connoisseurs" of the Catechism. So far as I know, nobody has observed that this question says almost the opposite of what its previous draft, the *Catechesis Minor* of Ursinus, said. In the *Minor* one reads: "Why do you add at the end of your prayer the little word Amen? Because I know that my prayers are as certainly heard by God as I truly desire this." In the Heidelberg Catechism we hear the final answer in its biblical depth and its almost Augustinian phraseology: "Amen means: this shall truly and certainly be. For my prayer is much more certainly heard by God than I *feel* in my heart that I desire such things from him." (Instead of "I am persuaded" as given in the 400th Anniversary Edition, I prefer "I feel"; see the German *ich füle* and the Latin *sentio*.)

The strength of my religious feeling falls behind my existential desires, and the strength of my desires falls far behind God's active attention to my needs: "For we do not know how to pray as we ought" (Rom. 8:26). "For God is greater than our hearts, and

The Catechism as an Expression of Our Faith

he knows everything" (1 John 3:20). How often in my pastoral life these wonderful words have enabled me to comfort people in doubt and temptation! Again and again we want to believe in our own belief and so are drawn toward the quicksands of introspection and, as a result of it, of despair. But faith is "Other directed." It clings to the "faithfulness" (Hebrew *amunah;* Greek *pistis*) of God; it is confidence in God's fidelity. Biblical faith is by definition self-transcendence, not as an autonomous act (Karl Jaspers) but by self-surrender. This is the real deliverance *from* our self, and so *of* our self.

The last question is the counterpart of the first. The Catechism begins with the only comfort. It has an existential approach to the gospel. And it ends by saying that the gospel is far more than its reflection in our existence. Only if we know this is our existence saved from existentialism and it finds its real, its divine, partner and the encounter which it needs in order to be liberated.

We have reached the end of our journey through the Heidelberg Catechism. Of the many excellent books that have come out of the Reformation and are now known only to specialists, the Heidelberg Catechism has best endured the centuries in the affection of church members. The secret of its success lies in its personal and existential approach. That approach has given this booklet a depth and warmth that enables it to stand unsurpassed among the Reformed and other confessions.

This approach, however, has its limitations. It pays full attention to the individual and his present comfort in God. As we have seen, this attention does not detract from the objective elements in Christian truth; but it cannot prevent some of those aspects which go beyond the present situation of the individual to suffer a certain setback. I mention as the two principal aspects those of ecclesiology and of eschatology. Question 54 on the church is excellent but far too short, and it is more interested in the invisible than in the visible side of the church. Of course the "I" who speaks here is not individualistic; he partakes in the faith of the whole catholic church. But the expressed wording of the Catechism does not do sufficient justice to this basic reality.

A similar remark can be made about eschatology. We remember

the moving words of Question 58. Nevertheless, the eschatological perspective plays but an additional and secondary role. So it is not surprising that Question 123 explains the words "thy kingdom come" mainly in terms of the present: "So govern us by thy Word and Spirit that we may more and more submit ourselves unto thee," and so on. We know that every approach to the infinite riches of God's love in Jesus Christ has its limits, which in the case of the Heidelberg Catechism are only the reverse of its qualities.

Thanks to its wonderful approach the Catechism of Heidelberg has maintained its relevance until the present day. When the famous preacher Herman Friedrich Kohlbrügge lay on his deathbed in 1875, he often exclaimed, "The Heidelberger, the simple Heidelberger! Stick to it, my children!" Some decades ago the Dutch theologian Oorthuys wrote an explanation of the Catechism under the striking title "The Eternal Youth of Heidelberg." When the representatives of the English Church at the Synod of Dort had returned home, one of them, Bishop Hall, reported: "Our Reformed brethren on the continent have a little booklet, the Heidelberg Catechism, whose single pages cannot be paid for even with tons of gold." The love for this Catechism will remain as long as there are people who seek their only comfort in our Savior, Jesus Christ.

Eduard Schweizer

•

SCRIPTURE AND TRADITION: THE PROBLEM

SCRIPTURE AND TRADITION: AN ANSWER

EDUARD SCHWEIZER is professor of New Testament at the University of Zurich.

CHAPTER SIX

Scripture and Tradition: The Problem

IMMEDIATELY AFTER HAVING FINISHED my studies I had to replace one of our most famous preachers, who had had a severe heart attack, and assume the pastoral work in a parish of 14,000 members in an industrial area of my hometown, Basel. This preacher had been well known everywhere in Switzerland and Germany for his outstanding sermons. And yet, the sharp tongues of the natives of Basel told me that the most difficult moment in his preparation of a sermon must have been the last when he had to search for a biblical text appropriate for his sermon. Such a procedure might be possible for an outstanding genius whose daily bread is the Bible, but certainly not for ordinary earthly beings like those of us who have to work for hours on the interpretation of our text before writing our sermon. However, the problem is not to be denied: What is the relation between scripture and denominational tradition, or between both of them and modern preaching?

THE NEW TESTAMENT EVIDENCE

Since even a space explorer at least starts from a territory well known to him, it is probably wise for me as a New Testament teacher to start from there. Our flight into the terrifying and not yet sufficiently explored areas of the problems about scripture and tradition will still be adventurous enough, and a safe arrival on the solid ground of an easy solution is not guaranteed to the passengers.

Scripture and Tradition: The Problem

The Importance of Tradition

Recent New Testament research detected how much even the earliest writings of our New Testament, the letters of Paul, owe to a still earlier tradition of the church. Paul himself stresses the fact that he handed down to the Corinthians what he in turn had received from the church, and that this is of first importance (1 Corinthians 15:3). Such tradition goes, through the intermediaries, back to Jesus himself (1 Corinthians 11:23). One of my students, W. Kramer, has shown in his dissertation,[1] how much Paul depends on earlier tradition even in his use of titles, such as the use of "Christ" in specific connections, or phrases such as the expression "in the Lord."

The *Formgeschichte* certainly proved the fact that even our earliest Gospel is a collection of pericopes handed down to Mark in an already traditional form. The Gospel of Matthew closes with the commandment of the risen Lord to create a tradition by teaching all nations what Jesus had commanded his disciples. Luke, in his preface, explicitly states that he went carefully through the tradition available to him. The second letter of John warns against anyone who goes ahead, and summons the church to abide in what it has heard from the beginning. The Pastorals call their readers back to the sound doctrine of Paul and fight those who have wandered away into vain discussions promoting speculations rather than the divine training (1 Timothy 1:4-6). There is no doubt that all New Testament authors emphasize that anyone who loses the connection with the original tradition will get lost like a child's balloon which is no longer held on its string.

The Importance of Free and Modern Interpretation

And yet, the same apostle Paul reinterprets his tradition to a great extent so that very often it says something quite different from its original meaning. One of the most striking examples is to be found in the preface of Romans.[2] One can prove by the style and vocabulary used there that Paul quotes an earlier creed proclaiming that Jesus, the Son of David according to the flesh, was made Son of God by his resurrection. This was understood as his enthronement and therefore, according to Psalm 2:7, as his adoption by God and the beginning of his regency. Simply by putting this creed into a new context, Paul interprets the divine sonship of Jesus as an eternal one, so that his resurrection gave him only a new power to exercise.

Similar results would be reached by comparing the formula quoted in 1 Corinthians 11:23 ff. and the Pauline doctrine of the Lord's Supper or the creed quoted in 1 Corinthians 15:3-5 and its interpretation by Paul which stresses only one point that was not central in the creed, namely, the reference to eyewitnesses of the resurrection. In 1 Corinthians 7:25 he admits that he has no command of the Lord for the problem in question, but given his own opinion, closing with the sentence: "And I think that I have the Spirit of God" (1 Cor. 7:40). Paul knows that in new situations, new interpretations or opinions are needed and must be given confiding in the presence of the Spirit of God.

According to the end of Matthew's Gospel the teaching of all nations seems not to be a mere repetition of the words of Jesus, since it is dependent on the promise that the risen Lord will be with them to the close of the age. Luke writes a second book after his Gospel and describes the development of the proclamation of Christ under the guidance of the Spirit, an enterprise considered half a century ago by F. Overbeck as being a worldwide display of bad taste.[3] The Fourth Gospel introduces a Jesus who speaks in an absolutely new manner, because he is actually the risen Christ and no longer the earthly Jesus. And in the Pastorals the ethics of the surrounding Hellenistic culture are taken over in a large way.

The New Testament itself summons its readers to keep carefully to the old, original tradition, and shows at the same time how impossible it is to keep this tradition unaltered. This is the problem with which we have to deal.

THE PROBLEM

Sola Scriptura—The Scripture Alone

The Heidelberg Catechism is part of a church tradition going beyond the limits of the New Testament canon. But every sentence in it, sometimes almost every word is buttressed by a pas-

Scripture and Tradition: The Problem

sage of the Old or New Testament. Whereas Martin Luther rejected James and Revelation, in the Heidelberg Catechism we even feel a concern to be fair toward all books of the New Testament and to quote all of them in the appropriate place. Hence the Heidelberg Catechism is an excellent example for the solution of our problem profered by the Reformation churches. While in the Roman Catholic Church scripture and tradition were of equal authority, in the Reformation churches scripture formed the sole authority, and the tradition was but an interpretation of the scripture. The question is whether this simple solution of the problem has not broken down today.

The understanding of the New Testament is dependent on our questions. Let us, as a test for this thesis, choose a very simple example. The main question of a pious Jew in Palestine was: "How shall I be saved in the last judgment?" The conception of such a judgment at the end of the times and the appearance of the heavenly Judge on the clouds of heaven was familiar to everyone. Therefore when someone preached, "Jesus, the Son of man, will come on the clouds of heaven," everybody understood correctly: it will be Jesus whom I shall encounter in the last judgment; my acceptance or rejection of his preaching will decide on my acceptance or rejection then. If, however, exactly the same sentence had been preached in Athens, any one of the hearers would probably have run home to tell his wife, "Listen, there is a man in the marketplace saying that a flying man will come, flying even over the clouds." And if his wife had asked him what man this would be, he would have answered, "Oh, one with a very foreign name that I could not remember, something like Jason." Thus, in Athens exactly the same word would have meant something totally different from what it meant in Jerusalem. This would have been so because the typically Jewish way of imagining eschatological events, namely the understanding of man's destiny in direct relation to this expectation of the last judgment, was unknown to the Athenean.

Or let us take the story of the centurion in Capernaum[4] who believed that Jesus could heal his servant without entering his house. The word of Jesus at the end of the pericope shows that the story calls the Jew to repentance because a Gentile showed such a strong faith whereas the Jews repelled Jesus. As soon as this story was told in gentile churches, it was almost inevitable that it became a call to boasting. Gentile Christians would have been tempted by it to do exactly that from which Jesus wanted to free his hearers. As the Jews boasted, "Our forefather Abraham believed in God, therefore we are elected and saved by God"; so gentile Christians were tempted to boast: "Our forefather, the centurion, believed, therefore we and not the Jews are now elected and saved by God." Church history and the persecution of Jews by Christians shows in what a shameful way the church succumbed to this temptation more than once.

Consequently, John in his gentile surroundings retells this story in a very different way. For I am convinced that the same story forms the background of the pericope about the official in John 4:46 ff. It was necessary for John to tell it differently lest it be transformed from a call to repent into a call to boast. The changing situation of the hearers changed the message of this story so that a mere literal repetition, orthodox as it might be, would lead to heresy, not to faith.

The message of a biblical saying or story is dependent on the questions which we have in mind when we tackle it.

There is a continuing revelation within the New Testament. Even more is to be said. "When the Spirit of truth comes, he will guide you into all the truth" (John 16:13). God's revelation did not stop with Jesus' death, not even with Easter or the fiftieth day after Easter. We have seen how the title "Son of God"[5] was interpreted in a new way in Paul's letters. It meant in Palestine a man elected by God and adopted into a close relationship to God, as it is said of the Israelite king: "You are my son, today I have begotten you" (Ps. 2:7). It meant in Greece a divine being begotten by a God. It meant in a Hellenistic–Jewish area, which was typical for most Christian congregations, probably a divine being coming from heaven like the logos of Philo, the firstborn son of God. The titles "Servant of God" and "Lord" were probably not applied to Jesus until after some development of the early church's preaching.

It took considerable time for the church to understand what

Scripture and Tradition: The Problem

Isaiah 53 had to do with Jesus, why Jesus had to die, or that the idea of preexistence could be applied to Jesus. The title Christ received a totally new meaning from the life and death of Jesus; however some time elapsed before this was really comprehended, and after still more time, in Hellenistic churches not familiar with the Jewish title, the newness of its meaning vanished again and the title became little less than a proper name.

Thus the New Testament certainly contains in itself quite a history of doctrines. It is not enough to say that it is merely a reinterpretation of the teaching of Jesus or even of the very first church, let us say, at Pentecost. There are new insights and new revelations. Paul's doctrine of God's grace justifying the Gentiles without a previous conversion to the law is undoubtedly a new revelation compared with the message of the Jerusalem church in the first years after Easter. Acts hence rightly describes new revelations after Pentecost, the one to Peter in Joppa or the command of the risen Lord to Paul (10:15, 19 f.; 9:6, 15 f.).

There is a continuing revelation of God within the New Testament, from the sayings of Jesus to the Apocalypse, Hebrews, and the second letter of Peter.

A canon within the canon is needed.[6] Let us begin with a relatively easy problem. The letter to the Galatians fights against an overevaluation of the law by which obedience to the law becomes a means of salvation. The first letter to the Corinthians fights against an overevaluation of the wisdom by which knowledge of all the mysteries becomes a means of salvation. In both cases the uniqueness of Christ the Savior is endangered. A preacher in a typically Jewish congregation in which salvation by works of the law was still the object of belief, would see Galatians as the center of his canon and admit that, of course, 1 Corinthians belongs also to the canon, since wisdom might play a similar role in other areas. A preacher in Greece, where the insight into the mysteries of the deity automatically brought salvation, would decide the other way around. The needs of the respective congregations urge the church to declare one letter as the center of its preaching and to read another letter only in the light of the first one, and urge another church to make a reverse decision.

In this case the difference between the two decisions would not be strongly felt, since the theological attitudes of both letters are fundamentally the same; both letters having been written by the same author. The difference lies more in the application of the same theological principle. But let us take the example of Romans and James. James does not deny that faith is required: "I by my works will show you my faith" (2:18); but he proclaims emphatically that the summons to good works must be the center of our message in which the call to faith is implied. Paul, in his letter to the Romans, certainly does not deny that the believer does good works: "I appeal to you, . . . by the mercies of God, to present your bodies as a living sacrifice" (12:1); but he proclaims equally emphatically that the very center of all Christian proclamation is the mere grace of God; and faith, our only salvation, from which all good works follow. Hence the same Old Testament passage leads Paul to declare that "to one who does not work but trusts him who justifies the ungodly, his faith is reckoned with righteousness" (Rom. 4:5), and James to declare contrariwise that "a man is justified by works and not by faith alone" (2:24). I do not assert that both statements are irreconcilable, but I do assert that we cannot dodge the decision as to whether we consider Romans 4 as the real center of the gospel and James 2 as a correction necessary in certain cases or do it the other way around. Do we declare that Paul is the real canon in the light of which the letter of James has to be read, or do we declare that James is the real canon whereas Paul's doctrine deals with exceptional cases?

Other similar decisions have to be made. If the Pastorals are the canon within the canon, the formation of an institutional church is the very center of the gospel, and other writings correct only some wrong excrescences of this principle. If, inversely, the Johannine Epistles are this canon, the free testimony of the Spirit is the one important feature of the church, and other writings only warn against a misuse.[7] If the genuine sayings of Jesus are this canon, the Sermon on the Mount and the call to discipleship are the main subjects of the church's preaching; if Paul's letters, the doctrine of justification. If Luke is this canon, a doctrine of *Heilsgechichte,* a mild synergism combined with some

Scripture and Tradition: The Problem

elements of divine grace, and the slow development to the early catholic church are the new insights of the Christian era; if John is the canon, it is the presence of the eschatological love of God, totally different from all that was before. Some of these alternatives may be misrepresented in the extreme brevity that is needed here, but the relevance of the problem is unmistakable.

Nobody is able to read the scripture without choosing a center in the light of which he reads all other parts of the Bible.

Different denominational traditions rightly claim the New Testament as their basis.[8] After what we have said about a canon, we may be brief here. For more than a decade some twenty German professors and one Swiss (namely, I) have dealt with the problem of the doctrine of the Lord's Supper. The result of the discussion was the formulation of eight theses on which both sides—Lutherans and Calvinists—agreed that everything which was really essential for the understanding of the Lord's Supper had been said in these theses.[9] This result became possible the moment that we turned to face all the New Testament evidence *against* our respective traditional position.

I remember well the manner in which E. Käsemann once formulated the agreement of all New Testament colleagues present at the meeting. He said that if the words of institution go back to Jesus himself, they were for him some kind of a parable, so that even Ulrich Zwingli could claim the authority of the words of institution as the basis of his doctrine. On the other hand, the same words meant much more for Paul or Mark, so that both Calvin and Luther understood them better when read in their Pauline or Marcan context.

But this issue becomes even more dangerous when we ask whether the Roman Catholic Church could not legitimate quite a number of its positions by an exclusive preference for Luke and the Pastorals in the New Testament canon. In Luke and the Pastorals there is certainly a trend toward an institutional church which guarantees the orthodoxy of the tradition. Although I do not think that the concept of an apostolic succession is to be found there, the trend toward such an institution is unmistakable.

Even if a church does not neglect any biblical book, the choice of a center in the light of which it reads the other books determines its understanding.

God's revelation continues after the New Testament. Can we really maintain the thesis that God's continuing revelation suddenly stopped after 2 Peter, or that, before this time, it worked in the canonical writings only? We know how many of them were disputed for centuries. Several of them were only accepted into our canon because they wrongly claimed to be written by an apostle, as is undoubtedly the case with 2 Peter. Several others that are no longer part of our New Testament were considered canonical for centuries by different churches, for instance, 1 Clement and Hermas. There is but one alternative: either we accept the fact that our canon is not infallible, but due to many lucky or unlucky chances of a very human church history; or we admit the decisions of the official church were infallible at least up to the fifth century and become more or less Roman Catholic.

The problem becomes still more difficult when we turn to the Old Testament canon. Here the fact is obvious that different churches have very different canons. If we want a fundamentalist guarantee of the canon, we must even stick to the thesis that not simply the church, but our own denomination, is infallible in its decisions, and that all other churches with different canons are wrong. Let us face the facts: It is ridiculous to assert that from Abraham up to Jesus there was a continuous revelation of God; that, even after Jesus' time, it went on for a bit more than a century; that even after this period it was still at work with the church's decisions about the canon, although no longer producing canonical writings; but that, after the fifth century, it reached an end beyond which nothing more happened.

Thus it seems that only one consequence can be drawn: God's revelation goes on in the tradition of the church.

Is God's revelation in the history of the church to be seen on the same level as that in Israel? It is evident that God's revelation in Israel, in the people that he elected, is different from God's manifestation in the universal history of our earth. If we were right in our deductions that God's revelation did not stop in the

Scripture and Tradition: The Problem

second or fifth century of our era, must we not conclude that the history of the church is on exactly the same level as that of Israel? The revelation of God preparing and interpreting, during Old Testament times, the coming revelation in Jesus Christ, cannot be more authoritative than the revelation of God interpreting his final revelation in Jesus Christ and guiding the church into all the truth by the presence of the Holy Spirit himself. Again, let us face the facts: Does it not follow that the only logical consequence would be to create a canon of this continuing revelation of God, parallel to the canon of the Old Testament, i.e., to create a tradition guaranteed by ecclesiastical approbation? Again, this would mean that we were to convert to Rome or to a church very similar to Rome.

And yet, appearances are deceptive. This seemingly logical consequence is not logical. The New Testament time and again impresses upon us the fact that there is a definite difference between the Israel of the Old Testament and the church of the New Testament: God's word became flesh in Jesus Christ; therefore every member of the church has the Spirit. Different as the views of the Spirit are in the various books of the New Testament, they all agree in this decisive fact: the Spirit is no longer given to outstanding persons for special tasks only; it is given to every believer.[10] For the incarnate Word of God is henceforth the definite canon by which to judge the revelation of the Spirit.

We agree with our Roman Catholic brothers: God's revelation goes on in the tradition of the church. In this respect Old Testament and church history are to be seen on the same level. But we disagree: there is no guarantee of an orthodox tradition by ecclesiastical approbation. The Spirit is given to every believer, and the only test to judge the tradition is the incarnate Word of God. But what does this mean?

Solus Christus—Christ Alone

One of the most illuminating characteristics of the Heidelberg Catechism is its Christocentrism. The Catechism begins in Question 1 with the statement that Jesus Christ is the unique consolation both in life and in death. When it teaches in Question 3 that we learn to know our wretchedness through the Law of God, it explains this thesis at once in Question 4: it is Jesus Christ who interprets the Law. The central part dealing with man's salvation is in fact a Christology. This Christological interest shapes also the third part. The answer of the first question in this section (Question 86) begins with Jesus Christ. He, not man, is the subject of our gratitude as well as of our salvation. This strict concentration on the praise of Christ's deeds enables the Catechism to deal in a really revolutionary way with the Ten Commandments in the third section only. This might well be the most stimulating new revelation in this catechism. The obedience of the church is the work of Christ himself not less than the redemption of the church.

There are different interpretations of Jesus Christ in the first kerygmatic formulas of the New Testament. Again it looks as if we had found a very simple answer to all our problems, namely, Jesus Christ himself as the yardstick for testing the continuing revelation of God in the tradition of the church. And again, appearances are deceptive. For at once the question arises: Who is Jesus Christ? Let us take the first Christological confession of faith: "Jesus Christ." Peter formulated it in Caesarea Philippi, but immediately afterward it became obvious that he had not understood at all what he had formulated so excellently. And Jesus said, "Get behind me, Satan! For you are not on the side of God, but of men" (Mark 8:33). The word Christ had evidently been understood by Peter quite differently from what Jesus himself or the church after Good Friday understood by this term. The same would be true, if we investigated the use of *kyrios* (Lord). In Palestine the term designated the one who guided the church, to whom it was obedient, and whom it expected as its judge. In Greece it designated the heavenly Ruler who had conquered all demons and heavenly powers so that whoever invoked his name was safe for all eternity.

The problem becomes more serious as soon as we consider more elaborate creeds, even of the pre-Pauline church. According to 1 Corinthians 15:3-5, Jesus is a human being, after his death raised by God. His importance lies in his atoning death for the sake of the sinners. His uniqueness is due to his eschatological position at

Scripture and Tradition: The Problem

the end of the times in fulfillment of the Scriptures. According to Philippians 2:6-11, Jesus is a heavenly being humiliating himself, so that his very life on earth is in and of itself a miracle, and exalted to an eternal lordship after his death. His importance lies in his position as the Lord over all powers, and his uniqueness is due to his heavenly origin.[11] The difficulty of the problem may be illustrated by a saying of Gregory Dix: "If the very first church in Jerusalem immediately after Easter had had to decide between Arius and Athanasius, it would have sided with the former. Nonetheless it was the latter only who defended in the fourth century what this church actually believed."[12]

A well-trained B.D. student today probably knows more about the historical facts of Jesus' life, death, and resurrection than, for instance, Paul. He has learned to distinguish between facts and legends without historical value, between historically reliable sources and writings, which rather proclaim the heavenly Christ in the garment of the earthly Jesus, than being interested in an accurate report of what happened. And yet, this does not enable him to get at the innermost truth of these events in a better and more reliable way than Paul.

Even the expression "Jesus Christ," let alone a formulation like "life, death, and resurrection of Jesus Christ," is open to many different interpretations, so that it is in need of the interpretation of the church to give it its meaning.

What is a historical fact? That the effect of a historical fact is not merely dependent on the fact itself, but sometimes even more on its understanding, its interpretation and reinterpretation, may be illustrated by a modern example. It is certainly a fact that the West of the United States has been conquered by the white settlers. What does this fact mean? Three reflections are necessary before we can answer this question:

1. Do we consider and narrate the history of these objective facts from the viewpoint of the Indians or of the white settlers? The result will be very different, even if we report exactly the same facts.

2. What view determines the choice of facts that seem important enough to be remembered and told? Maybe the really de-

cisive facts, for instance, an unknown schoolteacher who influenced unobtrusively, and therefore unnoticeably, thousands of early settlers, are totally forgotten, while many unimportant facts, for instance, some bloody battles, are still remembered.

3. Is it the historical fact, or is it the way in which it is presented today, for instance, in Western films, television programs, and songs, that really influences us? All three questions show the close connection between a historical fact, in the narrower sense of the word, and its tradition. A fact is effective only through its tradition. One may even ask if it be wise to speak of mere facts; we cannot know of any fact without our understanding, that is, without our interpretation which is always subjective.

Although we may go back in history as far as we want, we shall never reach the sheltered island of mere facts not yet lashed by the gales of different interpretations and reinterpretations.

Is not Jesus' own interpretation this longed-for refuge? There seems to be a simple solution to all our problems, perhaps too simple, too tempting. Why not declare the words of Jesus as the canon within the canon? This indeed seems to present itself like the god who in the Greek theater was sent down from some ingenious machine in order to solve all complications. Quite understandably, J. Jeremias presents this solution, and strangely enough, G. Ebeling and E. Fuchs who certainly fight with another wing of the army of theologians seem to come rather close to this solution in their recent writings.[13] Why not indeed?

A first consequence would be that the decision of the New Testament scholar about the genuineness of a word of Jesus would determine the doctrine of the church. The thesis then becomes inevitable that our modern understanding of Jesus is superior to that of Paul and John. No longer would the New Testament be the foundation of the church, but modern scholarship detecting the genuine nucleus within the New Testament.

Let us assume for a moment that, according to God's plan of salvation, this is the goal which the development of the church should have reached. What does it involve? Jesus certainly celebrated a last meal, but it is equally certain that he never baptized or spoke about baptism. If only the genuine words and

Scripture and Tradition: The Problem

deeds of Jesus are the standard to judge the tradition, some kind of a Lord's Supper would perhaps be possible, but not baptism. There are almost no words of Jesus about the Holy Spirit that are generally accepted as authentic. Is therefore the Holy Spirit of second or even of no importance in the life of the church? There are many scholars who think that Jesus never spoke about his death, and certainly not about his resurrection. Are therefore the death and resurrection of Jesus of no importance? The same is true for the concept of a church, for the acceptance of the Gentiles without circumcision, and for justification by faith. The facts of some of these concepts may be found in sayings of Jesus, but their foundation would be a very uncertain one, due to a difference of opinion about the genuineness of some words.

But let us assume once again that all this is the will of God, that this uncertainty is a blessed one, and that some of the central customs of the church must be revised. The most questionable consequence of such a position is yet another. If the genuine words and deeds of the earthly Jesus were *the* standard of all tradition, the whole development of the Christian church would have been wrong from the very beginning. For it is not only a historically understandable inability to distinguish between facts and legends that prevented the authors of the New Testament from presenting the genuine historical Jesus. The starting point for all of them is the Easter event, and this means the heavenly Christ, not the earthly Jesus.

Even our earliest Gospel, Mark, begins with the statement that it is the Christ, the Son of God, about whom Mark will write. Before saying anything else, he quotes the Old Testament promises which show that, with John the Baptist, the eschatological age of salvation has broken into time. Throughout his Gospel, Mark describes Jesus as the one who wants to reveal God, but is not understood, or is merely misunderstood. The crowd is not able to listen to an open preaching at all, so that Jesus is bound to teach in parables. Even his disciples to whom he explains all the parables and to whom he predicts his suffering, misunderstand him totally so that he dies with the call, "My God, why hast thou forsaken me?"—followed by a loud cry. It is the Easter event only that enables men to understand what happened.[14]

John repeats time and again that it is but the Spirit who gives the rebirth without which nobody can see who Jesus is, and that the Spirit, who guides us into all the truth, is given only after the death of Jesus.

For all four Gospels it is true that they are written in the light of Easter and the experiences of the Spirit after Easter. This explains how easily the church altered many sayings of Jesus. Not even the Lord's Prayer has been handed down without considerable alterations. They were, and I think rightly, not considered as changes of the truth but as the necessary adjustments to new situations. All this is even more evident in the earliest books of our New Testament, namely, the letters of Paul, since the apostle has almost no references to the words or the life of the earthly Jesus, except to his crucifixion.

Two more thoughts may clarify this. First, Jesus purposely avoided giving to his disciples a doctrine concerning his person and his work, lest they dodge a real encounter with him by merely taking over a new doctrine. For instance, the fundamentally correct title Christ was not understandable in its new meaning until after Good Friday. And only men who went through the catastrophe of this day, failing themselves, were able to confess afterward that Jesus was really the Christ.[15]

Second, it belonged to the state of humiliation that there were things that Jesus did not know. "Of that day or that hour no one knows, not even the angels in heaven, not the Son, but only the Father" (Mark 13:32). Gethsemane, with its prayer: "Abba, Father, all things are possible to thee; remove this cup from me," would not have been possible, if Jesus had known beforehand every step and every detail up to his glorious resurrection. Therefore I consider Bultmann's thesis[16] as fundamentally right, although some corrections are necessary, as we shall see, namely, that it is not of first importance whether Jesus considered himself to be the Messiah, but it is important that he *was* the Messiah.

Even the genuine words or deeds of Jesus do not procure for us a guarantee for testing the tradition of the church or its preaching today.

CHAPTER SEVEN

Scripture and Tradition: An Answer

THE CONCLUSION DRAWN from the essay "Scripture and Tradition: The Problem" was that it is no longer possible to consider the Bible as a kind of quarry out of which the church orders the foundation stones for its dogmatic buildings, the proof texts for its doctrinal statements. Even if we went back in history to the first creedal statements of the early church or to the genuine words of Jesus, it would be impossible to find a pure expression of the truth like some kind of distilled water cleansed from all foreign substances. Luckily enough this is so. For, as we know, distilled water, deprived of its minerals and salts, no longer quenches our thirst. A "distilled" truth, not affected by the way of thinking, the insights and errors, needs and hopes of its respective time, would be but an ineffable mystery available for godlike beings only, and of no help to us.

The truth encounters us in the body of the truth for the hearers of Jesus, for the Palestinian churches in A.D. 30, for the Hellenistic communities of the fifties, for the church in Rome in 400, for the Reformation time, for the church of 1963 in the U.S.A., and so on. All these truths are undoubtedly different, and yet only different bodies of one truth. What enables us to preach confidently the truth for our time and our country without going astray? Where is truth, and where is untruth?

EDUARD SCHWEIZER

HISTORY AND TRADITION

In a very condensed way the first answer of the Heidelberg Catechism gives the essential solution: The Christ who is my Lord today, accompanying me day by day, is the same who was crucified for me. The togetherness of the earthly Jesus and the heavenly Christ, of then and now, of the incarnate Word and the "still-living" word of God is underlined by this formulation. Frequently the Catechism, when referring to any event in the history of Jesus, adds the very modern question: "What is its use for me?" This stresses again the togetherness of historical event and its meaning for our time.

The Origin of the Tradition in Easter and Pentecost. The basis of the New Testament writings is, as we have seen, the Easter event. Even the Gospels are written in the light of Easter so that the earthly Jesus and the post-Easter Christ become one.

What does Easter mean? According to John 20:21-23 Easter is also Pentecost. On Easter Sunday the risen Lord breathes the Holy Spirit on his disciples and sends them into the world. But also for Matthew the Easter event is the beginning of the mission of the disciples, and the promise of the heavenly Lord to be with them to the close of the age is actually the gift of the Spirit. For Paul, seeing the risen Lord and becoming his apostle was the same event (1 Corinthians 9:1; Galatians 1:16). Luke is the only one who distinguishes between Easter and Pentecost, but even he sees the two events very closely connected; for it is the risen Lord who, on the day of Easter, gives the commandment of the proclamation of the gospel to all nations and the promise of the Spirit.

Easter is God's answer to all the questions put by the life and death of Jesus. In and of itself the death of Jesus is meaningless. Many a man died, even in a more crucial way. Many a man died because of a misjudgment. Many a man uttered even more impressive sentences when dying. But Easter was God's yes to this death. Easter proved to the scattered disciples that in this death God himself had acted, saving the world in fulfillment of all his promises. Even if we had the best sound film of a Jerusalem newsreel of the year A.D. 30 (or whatever it was), it would not help us much, since it could not show what really happened on this day.

Scripture and Tradition: An Answer

It is Easter only, it is the revelation of the Spirit that shows what really happened.

It is therefore absolutely appropriate when the author of Revelation introduces his letters to the seven churches as the words of Christ, just because they are the words of the Spirit. Hence the introductory formula always refers to the heavenly Christ, the closing formula to the Holy Spirit as the real author of these letters. Revelation only explicitly states what, in the Synoptic or Johannine tradition of the deeds and words of Jesus went on for decades. In new situations, the heavenly Lord, through his Spirit, explained his former words and reinterpreted them in a new situation. The authority of the heavenly Lord could certainly not be less than that of the earthly Jesus. Why, therefore, should the New Testament hesitate to formulate his words so that they meant in the very situation of the church of that time what they were to mean from the beginning? Probably nobody purposely and consciously altered the words of Jesus; they only heard them in such a way that they spoke directly to their own problems and their own time.

The New Testament never severs the earthly Jesus from the risen Lord. It is the risen Lord only who, speaking through the Spirit, gives meaning to the words or deeds of the earthly Jesus.

The Relation of a Fact to Its Understanding. Even in the area of physical facts, modern physicists know about the problems that we touched. The questions which we ask alter the result of an experiment. This is true even more in the field of history. There is evidently some difference, at least in degree, between facts in the area of history and human encounter, and facts in the area of physics. The role that our understanding plays is greater in the former area than in the latter. A cancer, for instance, has its effects whether we know about it or not. The malignancy can be removed by surgery, and the healing is not dependent on our knowing that it was cancer.

Quite differently, a deed of love usually has its effects on us only if we know about and interpret it, as it was meant. It is possible that someone love us for years without our knowing it. In this case such a love would not affect us or change our situation.

It is equally possible that someone do something for us out of mere love, but we misunderstand his motive and are driven into inferiority complexes or even hate. Therefore a historical positivism, which puts historical facts on exactly the same level as physical facts, is impossible. It forgets that, in the area of human encounter, the interpretation and understanding of a fact is sometimes even more important than the fact itself. We remember the example of the conquest of the West and its interpretation in American history, movies, and television.

This, I think, may help us to find our way toward a solution of the problem of "scripture and tradition." Let us choose a very simple example: Assume that a girl pays all the debts of her boyfriend because she loves him and wants to give him a new start. They get married. The problem of their matrimony will be how he copes with what his wife has done for him. His feelings of inferiority toward her may grow more and more. Even doubts may arise as to whether she really did it out of love, or perhaps out of sheer calculation. Hence, the task of this girl will be to accompany her husband in a continuing love in order to interpret her initial deed to him, and to bring it home to him. Years of a common life will teach this boy to understand the payment of his debts in the way in which it was meant, namely, as a deed of mere love.

A deed of love and the continuing interpretation by love belong closely together.

The Oneness of God the Son and God the Holy Spirit. Our first step is a comparatively easy one. As it is in our example, the same person who does the deed of love for her friend and who makes him understand this deed, so it is one God who, as the Son, speaks to us in his incarnate Word, and, as the Spirit, interprets this Word to us, so that it becomes meaningful for us. This is the truth of the Trinitarian concept of the church.

The saving events in the life, death, and resurrection of Jesus Christ, and the proclamation of these events which brings the church into being, are both the acts of the one God and cannot be separated from one another. "God was in Christ reconciling the world to himself, . . . and entrusting to us the message of recon-

Scripture and Tradition: An Answer

ciliation" (2 Cor. 5:19). "The Spirit of truth . . . will not speak on his own authority. . . . He will take what is mine and declare it to you" (John 16:13). According to all four evangelists, the Baptist announced Jesus as the one who will baptize with the Holy Spirit. Paul once even identifies the Lord and the Spirit (2 Corinthians 3:17) and, according to the seven letters of Revelation 2—3, the words of the Spirit are the words of the risen Lord.

Thus God acting in Jesus Christ and God acting in the whole tradition of the church as the Holy Spirit is one. However, this first easy step is like the step from the safe soil down to the frozen pond. It is very easy, since it goes down to the pond, but after this first step we are skating on ice, possibly on very thin ice. For as soon as we grant what we have said, two main problems arise: First, how do we distinguish the Spirit of God from so many other rather ungodly spirits? Second, if we succeed in doing so, is the authority of this Spirit higher when speaking in the first century within the New Testament than when speaking in the sixteenth century through the Heidelberg Catechism, and higher there than in the preaching of our church in 1963? (A discussion of these problems will follow.)

The interpretation of the living events in the tradition of the church, from the first preaching of the apostles to the preaching of the church today, is the work of the same God who acted in Jesus Christ.

DANGER OF BEING NOT MODERN ENOUGH

The Heidelberg Catechism is, in and of itself, an example of contemporary speaking, of a proclamation which is up to date. When it deals, for instance, in Question 80, with the Lord's Supper in continuous confrontation with the Roman Catholic Mass, this is part of a new tradition originating from the needs of that time. Or when it defines, in Question 30, faith in Jesus Christ as excluding any trust in saints or any other savior outside of Jesus Christ, this is certainly a new formulation in a then very modern way which sprang from the problems of that time. When it deals with the Ten Commandments in its third part, after the doctrine of salvation, it presents a most stimulating new tradition, different from both Roman Catholic and Lutheran understanding, and due to the necessary discussion with both of these churches. Is this the language of God's Spirit?[1]

The First Mark of the Spirit: His Affection for Modern Men. What is the standard to test the utterances of the Spirit and to separate right and wrong tradition? Are Holy Spirit and enthusiasm the same? Is the vehemence in which the Spirit appears the standard? Is it so that the more a prophet is convinced that he speaks in the name of God, the more he is to be believed? Or is the effect that he produces on his audience the decisive fact? Or is it the ecclesiastical approbation?

In the pre-Pauline church the Spirit was naïvely identified with an extraordinary power for healing, prophecy, and so on. This led, in Hellenistic congregations, to an extreme preference for ecstatic phenomena. The only alternative to this was an ecclesiastical institutionalism, as it was probably to be found in Jerusalem under James after the persecution in A.D. 44 and the departure of Peter. Paul was the first to reflect carefully on the nature of the Spirit of God, because he was forced to answer the questions of the Corinthians, who were unable to distinguish between the enthusiasm of the Holy Spirit and wild ecstacies produced by unholy spirits. In his answer Paul points to two main marks of the Spirit of God.

The first one is surprising: the Spirit speaks "for the common good" (1 Cor. 12:7). He speaks so that he "edifies the church" (1 Cor. 14:4). He speaks in such a way that every member of the church understands him (1 Corinthians 14:2, 6-12). This means: the Spirit of God is always directed toward contemporaries. He is always speaking in modern language. He does so because God wants to reach men, not some particularly trained men who, like the scribes in Jesus' time, are living in a past time, but ordinary men in this continually changing world. If this were not the case, it would be best to put the sermons of Paul and Peter on a tape recording and play them in our services, instead of training ministers who are, in spite of their expensive training, not always on the level of Paul and Peter. A sermon without the burning love toward modern men, a sermon in an outlived language,

Scripture and Tradition: An Answer

no longer understandable in a modern world, is probably no sermon of the Holy Spirit.

It is the sign of the Holy Spirit that he does not speak into the air, but in modern language to modern men, knowing their needs, their hopes, and their dangers.

His Criticism of a Petrified Tradition. "The written code kills, but the Spirit gives life," says Paul (2 Cor. 3:6). "We serve not under the old written code but in the new life of the Spirit" (Rom. 7:6). There is no doubt that Paul reads his Bible very carefully and that he finds the new life of the Spirit in this very Bible. Long passages of his letters are interpretations of scripture. But when the scripture is used, as it is used in a fundamentalist theology, in a legalistic way, it becomes the written code against which Paul fights so vehemently. Then a rigid law replaces the gospel; the death caused by a literal understanding replaces the life of the Spirit who interprets the scripture for our own time.

Paul opposes all legalism in his churches so severely because one of the most dangerous errors is that, by simply taking over old, orthodox formulations, we could take over the spiritual life which lies behind these formulations. Against some groups of Jewish Christians he fights vigorously for his thesis that, in his mission to the Gentiles, the history of salvation goes on, though it seems in contradiction to some words of Jesus literally understood.

Whatever the roots of the Johannine tradition may be, it is certain that it is a totally new interpretation of Jesus' words and deeds by the post-Easter Spirit, which has not much to do with a literal repetition of the sayings of Jesus. It is certainly the Jesus of Palestine, but speaking in a new language to a new situation.

Even Matthew who is rather close to the conception of a new law, and for whom Jesus is, first of all, the teacher of a new righteousness, is in many respects a new interpretation for new needs. Besides, it is exactly Matthew who emphasizes that the church has the power of binding and loosing (18:18), i.e., of creating new law or invalidating old law, and of forgiving or keeping sins.

Luke distinguishes different periods of a continuing history of

God, in which the Spirit leads the church to new insights. A petrified tradition that can no longer be developed by the living Spirit into new insights is legalism which kills instead of bringing into life, even if it consists of the genuine sayings of Jesus.

Hence, an orthodoxy which replaces the life in the Spirit by an acceptance of the historicity of biblical facts and a legal authority of biblical words or of creedal formulas would be the killing legalism against which Paul, and in their way also, John, Luke, and Matthew fight.

The New Quest of the Historical Jesus. The new quest of the historical Jesus is certainly not such an orthodoxy. It seems to be, on the contrary, a very modern and unorthodox approach. However, everything depends on the place that we give to such a quest within our theological thinking. Let me develop this a little bit. In the creed of the post-Easter church—Jesus Christ—the title Christ says who Jesus is. He is the one in whom God finally and once for all encountered the world and saved it. But equally well, the word Jesus determines the word Christ. It is a crucified man, rejected by Israel, who is this Christ, not the national king subjecting all Gentiles to his nation. It is therefore necessary that Jesus not remain a mere name without concrete content. If we understand the new quest in this way, it is indeed a most necessary reaction against a theology in which Christianity was in danger of developing into a mere doctrine without any historical roots.

However, this new quest of the historical Jesus seems to have quite a different goal for most of its representatives.[2] It seems to assume that modern men when confronted with a historical pre-Easter Jesus not yet presented in the light of the Easter event by believers who already see in him the Christ, would be led to detect in him the Christ of the New Testament. Jesus then becomes the first of the believers, the one who enables us to believe, who takes us into his own relation to God. If the quest of the historical Jesus is meant in this way, I think that it is a very modern way of petrification of a tradition. The only difference would be that it is not the tradition of a developed ecclesiastical orthodoxy, but the tradition of the genuine sayings of the historical Jesus.

Scripture and Tradition: An Answer

This would lead us into a new legalism by which Jesus becomes a mere ethical example and teacher. I cannot see why we then should go exclusively to Jesus and not to Socrates whose example and farewell discourses still move us, or to Epictetus who not only ate and drank with the socially low classes, but was a slave himself and helped thousands of slaves to bear their lot. Who would deny that Jesus was an outstanding teacher and example? He really helped men to believe and led them to God, and all this is important and helpful. But this does not distinguish him basically from other helpers, teachers, and examples. The one fact which distinguishes him from all others is—according to all books of our New Testament—Easter.

When the New Testament creates the new phrase "believing *in* Jesus Christ," when it speaks so often about "believing *that* Jesus Christ was crucified and raised from the dead," it means much more than believing because he helped us to believe. Therefore all the Gospels presuppose the Easter event from the beginning and depict the earthly Jesus in its light, as we have seen. Therefore the tradition was never anxious to hand down the words of Jesus without any alteration. For was it not the risen Christ himself who interpreted his former words by the very fact of his resurrection or by his lordship over the church after Easter? "His disciples did not understand this at first; but when Jesus was glorified, then they remembered" (John 12:16). This faith can only be experienced, lived, witnessed to, but it cannot be deduced from a no longer possible historical reconstruction of a pre-Easter Jesus. Historical facts never create faith; only faith creates faith.

The starting point for all Christian proclamation is the faith that Jesus is the Christ, crucified for us, raised by God, not simply teacher and ethical example. The quest of the historical Jesus is a second step only which prevents this belief from becoming a mere idea without a basis in real facts within history.

DANGER OF LOSING ROOTS IN HISTORY

One of the most startling explanations of the Heidelberg Catechism is "born of the Virgin Mary" in Question 35. For the whole stress of the Catechism lies on the real human nature of

Jesus who, born of the flesh and blood of the Virgin Mary, became equal to his brothers in every respect except sin. In Question 44 Jesus' descent to hell is interpreted as his anguish on the cross, and Question 47 states, in a way not less questionable than that of the Lutheran thesis of that time, that the human nature of Christ is now in heaven and no longer on earth. We could also point to Question 37 which interprets the word suffered as including the whole earthly life of Jesus, to Question 41 in which the burial of Jesus is understood as the proof for the reality of his death, to Question 16 which emphasizes his human as well as his divine nature, and to others. It is evident that the Catechism wants to stress the roots of all Christian doctrine in the historical life and death of Jesus.

The Second Mark of the Spirit: His Testimony to Jesus. The other standard for judging utterances of the Spirit which Paul mentions is the testimony to Jesus the Lord. Whoever witnesses to Jesus as the Lord is moved by the Spirit, and whoever denies this is far from the Spirit of God (1 Corinthians 12:3). It is even possible that this verse is explicitly directed against Docetists who saw in Christ simply a heavenly idea unconnected with a real human person in history. Be this as it may, it is evident that for Paul the Spirit of God is not only directed toward contemporary men, but also toward the one fact in which God revealed himself to the world, once for all.

Christianity, unlike all other religions, is shaped by the fact that the preached word of God is but the vehicle by which the incarnate Word of God meets us. If we lose this basis in history, we shall have lost the content of the gospel. God is not to be restricted to his actual speaking in the preaching of our time. His Word to the world is a man of flesh and blood, so real that he was hanged. A spiritualized preaching, severed from the history of Palestine in the first three decades of our era, would be like a tree whose roots were pulled out of the soil which gave it life. Jesus Christ is God's incarnate Word, unchangeable, not subject to translation in ever new languages.

Therefore the gospel is understood, not as a doctrine about eternally unchangeable ideas, but as the praising proclamation of

Scripture and Tradition: An Answer

God's deed, which in Jesus Christ once for all changed the situation of the world.

The Affinity of the Spirit to History and Tradition. In exactly the same position in which the law and a rigid legalism are found in Galatians, do we find the wisdom in 1 Corinthians. To such a wisdom Paul opposes his preaching that knew nothing except "Jesus Christ and him crucified" (1 Cor. 2:2). The Corinthian wisdom was obviously a presentation of quite a number of Christian thoughts without being a proclamation of the shocking historical fact of the crucifixion of Jesus. For Paul himself, this fact was so scandalous that he was never in danger of forgetting that Jesus was a real, historic person. But, of course, this was different for Greek congregations that were living far away from the historical facts of about A.D. 30 in Jerusalem. They were in real danger of developing into Gnosticism as we know it from groups of the second century.

Gnosticism presents a comprehensive doctrine of salvation, containing even a myth which tells of the descent from and the ascent to heaven of a manlike savior, but here, only the kerygma matters. The myth is but an illustration of the eternally unchangeable truth. Therefore it does not matter at all whether uneducated people believe that all this really happened in distant primitive times, or more educated people take this myth as a mere image for the truth. Against such tendencies John formulates what Paul had written in a simpler form in 1 Corinthians 12:3: "Every spirit which confesses that Jesus Christ has come in the flesh is of God, and every spirit which does not confess Jesus is not of God" (1 John 4:2-3).

Even more important is the fact that, when some time had elapsed and the real historical figure of Jesus of Nazareth was in danger of fading away, four Gospels were written in order to defend the gospel against being converted into Gnosticism. The historical facts are nothing without their interpretation by the post-Easter Spirit and therefore all the Gospels present the earthly Jesus in the light of the risen Christ. However, this interpretation, in and of itself, is equally meaningless if not understood as the interpretation of these facts.

The New Testament writers are not concerned with a distinction between the so-called historical Jesus and the risen Lord speaking through the Spirit, but they are certainly concerned with the distinction between a mere doctrine or a mere myth and a history interpreted by the Spirit.

The Kerygmatic Theology. When New Testament scholarship detected that the real interest of the evangelists was essentially the same as that of Paul and other authors of letters, namely to proclaim Jesus as the Christ, to preach rather than to give an accurate historical report, a seemingly easy solution of all problems presented itself. The kerygma, the proclamation of Jesus as the Christ by the post-Easter church, was the sole center of the gospel. The mere "that"[3] of the existence of a man Jesus, namely that he really lived and died, was sufficient.

This is perhaps not wrong, since Paul, in all his letters, does not say much more than this. And yet, in this extreme formulation, it is at least open to severe misunderstandings. For the very content of this proclamation of the first church was the fact that God's saving act happened in the life, death, and resurrection of Jesus, that it was not a new doctrine, but an event within a definite period of time and a definite geographical area, that God's redeeming Word consisted of flesh and bones, and not only of syllables. Hence, this event must, for the believer, mean more than a mere name.

That the bearer of this name proclaimed the kingdom of God, called to repentance, urged disciples to follow him, healed and preached in an astonishing way, did not look for security but went into the center of danger and had to go through the anguish of a shameful execution before rising from the dead—all this is extremely important, lest the proclamation of the saving act of God fade into a theory about God. It is unimportant whether or not all the stories told in the Gospels happened. But it is important that Jesus is, for us, not a mere spirit, but a man with specific features. There is quite a difference between an image with many details uncertain, and a vague idea which is not much more than a mere name.

Let me give an illustration. Assume that we had to write the history of the Christianization of some heathen country. We could describe one outstanding conversion. Everything would be historically accurate. And yet the book would be absolutely deceptive. There would be nothing about all the defeats, the mistakes, the sins, the hypocrisy and apostasy which also took place.

We could do it in another way. Granted that we knew about all the highlights and the deep shadows of this history, that we really had investigated everything, we could choose one average family of that country and describe what happened. We could invent their names and describe in the example of this one family what happened in thousands of different families. It would be fiction, and yet this would be the truth. The historical accuracy alone does not decide, but the deep understanding of what happened. Yet it is important that, even in this fictitious family, we recognize the real events, the main features of the history which passed there.

A theology in which the kerygma of the first church is the center must be corrected by the insight that this very kerygma proclaims that a man of flesh and blood in his concrete life and death and resurrection is the mystery in which God encounters the world.

JESUS CHRIST, THE NEW TESTAMENT, THE TRADITION, AND THE CHURCH TODAY

The redaction of the Heidelberg Catechism was teamwork. We are not even sure who the final editor was. There was a long period of discussion and revision of earlier drafts. More than that, it was an ecumenical work; catechisms of both Lutheran and Reformed tradition were compared.[4]

The Third Mark of the Spirit: A Gift to the Whole Church. According to Paul, it is extremely important that the whole congregation understands the message of the Spirit and is able to agree with its "Amen" (1 Corinthians 14:16). Therefore the prophet speaking in the Spirit must be judged by the congregation (1 Corinthians 14:29). Different though the views of the the Spirit are in the New Testament, all agree on this point: the Spirit is given to all believers. "Anyone who does not have the

Spirit of Christ does not belong to him" (Rom. 8:9). "You shall receive the gift of the Holy Spirit. For the promise is to you and your children and to all that are far off, everyone whom the Lord our God calls to him" (Acts 2:38 f.).

In the New Testament, the Spirit is never an individual gift to outstanding religious geniuses. It is always the gift to the whole church. This means that the preaching of the Spirit is subject to control by the members of the church. Because of this I always prepare my sermons together with a group of church members, listening for an hour and a half to their discussion of the text.

The Spirit is given to the church and is therefore controlled by all the brethren (and sisters, of course).

The Role of Tradition. God cannot contradict himself. Therefore we must listen carefully to all our brothers and, if we disagree, ask ourselves whether we are not hard of hearing to the voice of the Spirit. But the church did not start in 1963, and the Spirit did not begin to speak in 1963. There are brothers throughout all the centuries of church history. Some of these brothers are in an outstanding position. They have suffered and died for the truth that they proclaimed, and/or they have proclaimed that truth not as individuals but as the church, in common agreement. This is the case, for instance, with the declaration of Barmen in the confessing church of Germany in 1934, or with the Heidelberg Catechism in 1563.

This is one reason for listening to the tradition, but there is another one. Past centuries had their own way of thinking. On the one hand, being men of another century we are usually quite aware of the errors which were involved in their thinking. In the discussion of the Lord's Supper, for instance, Lutherans and Calvinists thought in categories totally foreign to the New Testament, because they had a conception of matter or substance conceived in the Middle Ages but unknown in New Testament times. Hence it goes without saying that we must read the tradition with a critical mind, avoiding their inappropriate categories of thinking as far as possible.

On the other hand, being men of our century, we are usually blind to the inappropriate categories of our own century. And

Scripture and Tradition: An Answer

here, the tradition renders us the most necessary service of helping us to see the limits of our own thinking. It may, for instance, be impossible for us to repeat literally the clause in the first answer of the Heidelberg Catechism that Jesus Christ paid with his blood completely for my sin and redeemed me from all power of the devil. And yet, it reminds us that there is a dimension in the New Testament message which is not yet covered, if we consider Jesus mainly as a teacher or ethical example or even the messenger of justification by faith.

It is the advantage of tradition that we, while better aware of its limits and errors than of those of our contemporary thinking, may see in its light the deficiencies of our own theology.

The Role of the Scriptures. What is the particular position of the New Testament within this tradition? A first answer would be that what is true for the Heidelberg Catechism or the declaration of Barmen, is true to a greater extent for the New Testament. It is surrounded by a cloud of martyrs who died witnessing to its truth; it is teamwork in an excellent way, and its acceptance by the whole church is without parallel. However, all this is only a difference in degree.

A second answer starts from the fact that the New Testament distinguishes the first encounter of the risen Lord with the apostles clearly and definitely from later visions by which the heavenly Lord gives some guidance to the believer. Paul's encounter with the risen Lord near Damascus is the basis of all his preaching and is referred to in Galatians 1:16 and in 1 Corinthians 9:1, also in Romans 1:1 and similar places. The vision of 2 Corinthians 12 with its extraordinary ascent to heaven should not be mentioned at all since it is a mere personal experience without any importance for the church as a whole. Luke draws a strict borderline between the appearances of the risen Lord within the first forty days and heavenly visions like the one Peter had in Joppa and even Paul's in Damascus.

We have said that God is both acting in Jesus Christ and in the Spirit interpreting and actualizing these events. It is evidently the understanding of the New Testament that Easter belongs to the "once for all" of God's deed of salvation. As in any deed of love between men, the deed of love and the interpretation of the deed by love, which transforms a past event into a present reality, are inseparable. God himself acts in Jesus and gives the understanding of his acts, so that they become present. Easter is the event which always reminds us that there is but one understanding of God's acts in Jesus Christ, and that it is God himself who gave us this understanding, once for all, unchangeable in its essence. The Word of God is the incarnate Word, not the mere actual spoken word, yesterday this way, today that, and tomorrow still different.

The New Testament is certainly not identical with this understanding that God himself gave to men. It is written in Greek, and every human language necessarily involves quite a lot of categories of thinking which are partly appropriate and partly inappropriate for expressing the divine truth. It was written by men who understood and misunderstood what God wanted them to understand. And yet, the New Testament is, first, historically the closest to the event of the incarnate Word of God. Second, it has been tested time and again by the whole church. Third, it stood the test in the sufferings of the church before and after its acceptance as the canon of the church. Fundamentally it does not lie on another level than all teaching of the Spirit throughout the history of the church. However, this would be a merely theoretical thesis. Theoretically also a gentle stroke on the hand of a child is the same as a whipping which leaves him crippled, since both are fundamentally corporal punishment; but actually there is all the difference in the world between the two.

The New Testament is part of the tradition, therefore necessarily expressed in human language, limited by contemporaneous possibilities of understanding, imperfect; and yet standing in a unique position as the beginning of the tradition, historically close to the incarnate Word of God, and the sign for its "once-for-all-ness."

CONCLUSIONS

It is an astonishing fact that the Heidelberg Catechism contains no doctrine of the authority of the scripture and yet bases every sentence on it. Questions 83-85 reject the Roman Catholic concept of the Pope as the bearer of the keys to heaven, but establish the idea of the whole church as executing the ministry of the keys.

Faith, not unlike love, lives without having guarantees. If a husband hires a private detective and gets his written reports which prove the faithfulness of his wife, it is not the beginning but the end of his love. Faith that requires guarantees is no longer faith. There are witnesses, there are signs, there are experiences, but there are no guarantees which would relieve us of believing. It is most illuminating that the first canon was created by Judaism, as soon as it had parted definitely from Christianity. The canon becomes a petrified tradition no longer able to create any life, as soon as it is considered as the guarantee of the orthodox truth. But if it is not a new law, a guarantee which could be taken over literally in a new legalism, it is the outstanding testimony of the contemporaries of the incarnate Word, tested and accepted by the whole church.

The canon is a fact, an event which gives us no guarantee, but which has proved its power and reliability. Except for a few short sayings attributed to Jesus and handed down outside of the New Testament, e.g., "Whoever is close to me, is close to the fire,"[5] there is nothing which could earnestly be considered as worth including in our New Testament. It might be that we could do without, for instance, the letter of Jude; but no church would dare to exclude a book from the canon, and I think we are glad that Luther did not exclude James and Revelation, as he at first would have liked to have done.

A sermon which earnestly tries to interpret its biblical text gives, of course, no guarantee that this message is really understood and that it offers us that bread which God wants to give us today, but it is at least an earnest attempt to listen to those witnesses to whom God spoke, before he spoke to us. It is at least a help that can free us from our own favorite thoughts that are not always identical with the thoughts of God. In a similar way it is wise for the church to listen carefully to its tradition, as it is handed down, for instance, in the Heidelberg Catechism. Again, a repetition of its formulas does not guarantee that we mean the same as they meant in their time, let alone that this meaning is the unsurpassable truth. But again, it is at least a remedy against an individualism which sees nothing beyond the limits of its own personality or its own time.

We shall certainly read the Scriptures and read the Catechism as men of our century. We shall translate the message of the New Testament into the needs of our time. We shall not forget that the ecumenical movement is God's gift and challenge to our time. Hence we shall not consider the Heidelberg Catechism as an exclusive possession of our denomination. We shall interpret it in such a way that other denominations are also able to understand its intention, and we shall also listen carefully to similar documents of other denominations. But we shall listen to the Scriptures and to our tradition; we shall listen humbly and intensely ten times before speaking once.

On the one hand, whoever possesses guarantees has got salvation in his own possession. No longer is he forced to ask questions and to pray for an answer. No longer is he entirely thrown on God alone. No longer is he a poor beggar expecting everything from his Lord. On the other hand, whoever believes in nothing but his own spirituality has equally got salvation in his own possession. No longer is he forced to listen except to himself. No longer does he know a God outside of his own soul, an incarnate Word of God, and a word given to a church which is greater than he. He too no longer is a poor beggar expecting everything from his Lord.

Luther distinguished between "certitude" and "security." Faith knows no security, because security means a guarantee of which we could dispose, a guarantee in our own hands. Security needs no God. But faith knows certitude, that last peace which knows that God is absolutely trustworthy, and that he will give us anew every morning what we do not possess.

The Heidelberg Catechism closes in an extraordinary way with the section on prayer. It is, according to Question 116, the main part of our gratitude, the best that can be said of man and his work. Whoever prays needs no other security or guarantees, but is not restricted to his own spiritual wisdom either. "Amen means: this shall truly and certainly be. For my prayer is much more certainly heard by God than I [feel] in my heart that I desire such things from him" (Question 129).

Howard G. Hageman

•

THE CATECHISM IN CHRISTIAN NURTURE

HOWARD G. HAGEMAN is minister of the North Reformed Church, Newark, New Jersey.

CHAPTER EIGHT

The Catechism in Christian Nurture

COMMENTARIES ON the Heidelberg Catechism by men like Karl Barth, K. H. Miskotte, or most recently André Péry, have been a welcome relief from the clumsy and wooden expositions which were produced in the nineteenth century. It says much that at last in the twentieth century we are able to read the Heidelberg Catechism as a document of the Reformation, that we have abandoned the attempt to make it express the theology of Westminster or Dort.

But welcome as this change of interpretation and this revival of interest are, I seriously question how far they have penetrated to the average communicant of the average congregation and how far they still remain the preserve of the theological specialist. I am not aware, for example, of any great revival of the use of the Catechism in my own communion, even though any domine who questioned it publicly would find himself facing an ecclesiastical court-martial before he could sing the *Gloria Patri!* This ardent defense of the Catechism as a piece of orthodoxy and this stubborn refusal to use it as a living instrument in the church pose a problem for one who would think of the Heidelberg Catechism as an instrument of Christian nurture. Is the Catechism an unrealized potential with possibilities which we may not hitherto have recognized?

The Catechism in Christian Nurture

NEGLECT OF THE CATECHISM

Let us begin with some negatives, with a brief cataloging—if not analysis—of some of the reasons why the Heidelberg Catechism has suffered neglect as an instrument of Christian nurture.

Outdated Language

The first reason may seem to be a minor one and happily it has now been corrected. But we must face the fact that until the 400th Anniversary Edition appeared late in 1962 our English translations were abysmally dated. Having been made, all of them, in the eighteenth or nineteenth centuries, in style and vocabulary they were heavy and cumbersome. Put before any young person—or for that matter, any adult of average American education and intelligence—the Catechism seemed to be a forbidding document with ecclesiastical jargon through which he was unwilling to wade. In the case of the official English version of my own church there were even some inaccuracies in translation, though I do not honestly suppose that that ever was a major deterrent to its use.

But the fact that we kept the Catechism attired in eighteenth-century knee breeches or nineteenth-century hoopskirts was an effective means of preventing its living in the twentieth century. That apparently nobody was concerned for a long time to give it a twentieth-century dress says much for the general estimate that we had of its usefulness.

That situation, as I have already observed, has now been corrected. The new English translation by Allen O. Miller and M. Eugene Osterhaven under the sponsorship of the World Alliance of Reformed and Presbyterian Churches is worthy of careful reading and study. I mean no disrespect to the greatness of this work when I say that I am still waiting for a further publication, the issuance of what I might call a J. B. Phillips version which would frankly paraphrase what cannot really be translated. To take a single illustration, the word comfort in Question 1 is not a very significant word and can be misleading. I do not question the wisdom of the translators in retaining it; there is no single word in English that will answer the need. I know; I have been looking for one for the past fifteen years. But the willingness to paraphrase rather than translate would open several possibilities.

For Children

A second reason for the neglect of the Catechism is that we have conceived of its use entirely in terms of instruction for children or, at best, adolescents. When you add the already noted difficulty in translation to the more important fact that the Heidelberg Catechism is not a juvenile work, you can easily understand the results. Many ministers and teachers, realizing the incomprehensibility of the material so far as their pupils were concerned, simply gave up and looked about for something easier. And many adults, having been dragged through the Catechism without ever understanding it—their sole recollection of the exercise being that they had to recite ten questions perfectly before the Consistory or, worse still, the congregation—put it away when they put away childish things.

I confess that I am depending here upon the memories of many persons with whom I have talked and that my statistical sampling is probably too small to warrant my conclusion. But I gather that a generation ago when the Catechism was still in general use, it was entirely limited to the instruction of twelve- and thirteen-year-olds and that the goal was to train them to recite a portion of it perfectly. I have yet to find an exception to my experience.

When I mention the Heidelberg Catechism, the eye brightens as at the recollection of an old friend, long since departed. "The Heidelberg Catechism? Oh, yes, I remember that. I still remember how frightened I was when I had to recite my questions before the elders!" But when I ask about any use of it since that distant time, I find there has been none. And when I ask about its content or meaning, except for vague replies about God or Jesus, I might as well be inquiring about the contents of the *Oxyrhynchus Papyri*. I conclude, therefore, that our use of an outmoded translation as a manual of instruction for children has resulted in the present neglect.

Impartation of Information

But I have saved until last the most significant reason, though what I have just said leads directly to it. We have conceived of

The Catechism in Christian Nurture

the role of a catechism as the impartation of information. The purpose of a catechism is to give the content of the Christian faith, preferably in as bald a form as the mathematics table. For fear that I was relying too heavily on my own impressions, I looked up the word in the *Oxford Dictionary of the Christian Church,* only to discover the following definition: "Catechism (from Gk. κατηχεω, 'to make hear,' hence 'to instruct'). A popular manual of Christian doctrine."

I admit that words like "instruction" and "doctrine" may be given another interpretation. But in the Reformed tradition for centuries the standing interpretation of them was entirely intellectual. It was essential, from our point of view, that our people know our doctrines exactly as they know the arithmetic tables. The Catechism was the instrument chosen for the job. Theological information was seen as the chief, if not the only, purpose of Christian education; and the Catechism was the means by which it was imparted. Indeed, I suspect that that is still the understanding of the purpose of the Catechism in many quarters of our churches, if not in a majority of them.

Well, we live in an era—some would say at the end of an era—in which that understanding of Christian education has been, to put it mildly, unfashionable. In fact, there was a time when it almost seemed as though the imparting of any kind of knowledge or information was considered the last purpose in Christian education, an unjustifiable invasion of the integrity of the young personality, a serious arresting of his own religious development.

I have no interest in getting into the rights and wrongs of the theory. My interest here is in pointing out that because any catechism was seen as the principal agent of this deficient and even perverted scheme of Christian education, all catechisms—the Heidelberg included—became the principal targets and the principal victims of the new school of Christian pedagogy. I have no desire to single out John Dewey as the chief assassin of the Heidelberg Catechism. But I have no hesitation in claiming that the philosophy of Christian education which resulted from Dewey's theories gave it its death blow in our churches. I hasten to add, however, that not all of the blame can be put there. By the interpretation of the Catechism and the use of it which had been current in orthodox Reformed circles for decades, we made it a perfect sitting duck for the destruction when it came.

CHRISTIAN NURTURE

If what I have said can be accepted as an adequate summary of our state of affairs and at least a partial explanation of what made us this way, our first positive task would seem to be an examination of exactly what we mean by *Christian nurture*. While it would be presumptuous of me, a parish minister, to attempt any full or final definition of the phrase, I should like to suggest what I consider to be several important ingredients in it and then proceed to look at the Heidelberg Catechism in the light of these suggestions.

Christian Knowledge

At the risk, then, of falling under the ban of the very school of Christian education to which I have referred, I should like to begin by saying that I cannot see how Christian nurture can avoid the element of information, can refuse to face the question of knowledge. After all, the Christian faith is not anybody's guess about the meaning of the universe or anybody's reaction to the demands of existence. It is a rather definite body of information which can be put in simple declarative sentences. We may disagree as to the number of declarative sentences which our summaries should include. We may even disagree as to their literal or metaphorical character. But unless we are prepared to admit that Christianity is a totally private experience which is completely incapable of being communicated, we have to say, it seems to me, that there is such a thing as Christian knowledge and information which can be taught exactly as other disciplines of learning can be summarized and taught.

In the lay world in our churches there is still a fright of such words as "doctrine," "dogma," and "theology." I have even had laymen put to me questions of the most profound theological dimensions while prefacing their inquiry with words like, "I am not interested in theology but why . . ." We have paid a heavy price in our churches for the assumption—still too readily made —that Christianity was exclusively pious feelings and good conduct, that the Christian faith was a formless, shapeless thing which every man could and should mold for himself. It may well be that our Reformed fathers dealt so exclusively with skeletons that the faith never came alive. But I am persuaded that one of the great reasons why the Reformed faith is so strangely unable to walk in this world is that it has no bones, that we have too much religion without a theology.

I make no apology, therefore, for asserting that in the first instance Christian nurture means instruction in the content and meaning of the Christian faith. The question I have to ask is how adequately any given instrument presents this content and meaning. Does it omit anything that is essential? Or does it possibly add material which is not really essential? Does it interpret the faith in a narrow and sectarian manner? Does it present as articles of faith things which are really matters of speculation? These are the criteria by which any judgment of any instrument of Christian nurture must begin. To pass over these as if they were irrelevant or to imply that the method of teaching is more important than the content is to betray one of the fundamental ideas of Christian nurture.

But at the same time I think that the protest against the sterile intellectualism and dogmatism of at least a certain section of the Reformed tradition was not without its point. *"Non intellectu salvum facere populum suum placuit Deo,"* said Ambrose. And there are many ways in which the Reformed tradition would have done well to have heeded his point. Christian nurture must involve something more than information. Even though our neglect of this something more is no excuse for our rejection of the intellectual element, the didactic motif, we do need to think more carefully about it than we have in the past. J. D. Benoit makes this point in a lecture on preaching:

> This, it seems to me, is the great lack in our preaching; it does not nourish souls. It does not take them by the hand, so to speak, and bring them to God, but always leaves them in the same situation, that of the morning after confirmation. It does not address itself to their spiritual development.... It is the pastor who must distribute the bread which makes souls live and grow spiritually.[1]

Personal Involvement

What Professor Benoit has to say about preaching is equally applicable to teaching. An instrument of Christian nurture should not only offer information, but it should present it in such a way that it becomes possible for the doctrine to involve the whole person. I suppose that this is what our fathers were getting at when they used to speak about "saving knowledge." By their very use of the phrase they indicated their realization that intellectual information was not enough, however we may criticize their implementation of their awareness. Christian nurture demands that doctrine always is seen in the light of personal relationship and personal commitment. After all, nurture implies growth. A fact cannot grow; a personal relationship is always capable of expansion whether in depth or breadth or height. We should want an instrument of Christian nurture therefore which, while adequately presenting the content of the Christian faith, presents it not as book learning but as personal involvement.

I think I must add that there is a nice relationship between book learning and personal involvement which is often overlooked. Indeed, I am aware of a tendency among us to play one off against the other as though they were mutually exclusive alternatives. Has not the story of the Reformed churches largely been the story of the warfare between the two—the pietist insisting upon personal involvement; the dogmatist insisting upon theological orthodoxy? The statement of the faith is never a substitute for personal involvement. But it is extremely important that we know the total dimensions of that with which we are involved. Rightly presented, an adequate statement of the faith is always a challenge to deeper involvement and therefore to greater growth. Any Christian nurture which insists upon the one at the expense of the other is bound to be deficient.

The Christian Community

But to these two ingredients I think that we, perhaps more than any other generation since the time of the Reformation, would want to add a third: Christians are not nurtured in isolation, but in community. No one, I think, can look at the New

The Catechism in Christian Nurture

Testament honestly and say that the goal of Christian nurture is personal religious development or individual religious maturity.

In the New Testament the goal of Christian nurture is always the edification of the church—the upbuilding of the body of Christ. "So shall we *all* at last attain to the unity inherent in our faith and our knowledge of the Son of God—to mature manhood, measured by nothing less than the full stature of Christ. . . . He is the head, and on him the whole body depends. Bonded and knit together by every constituent joint, the whole frame grows through the due activity of each part, and builds itself up in love" (Eph. 4:13, 16, N.E.B.).

This is not merely a matter of saying that we must see to it that our instrument of Christian nurture contains an adequate presentation of the doctrine of the church and seek to involve us in it. It goes much deeper than that. What I am trying to say includes at least two things. First, any adequate instrument of Christian nurture must assume the Christian community as the context in which it is to be used. Catechisms, if they are to be adequate instruments of Christian nurture, are not manuals of doctrine for little pagans; they are food which nourishes only inside the community. This is an extreme statement, but I think I could defend it. A good catechism would be nonsense if it were read by the man in the street; its assumptions would be meaningless to him. This is not to say that we do not need propaganda which will attract him. We do, and in much better quality than we seem to have. But it is to protest against the frequent confusion which we make between propaganda for the pagan and nourishment for the person within the community. The sad result of our confusion is that the pagan spits up what we hand him while the person within the fellowship is spiritually starved.

A second consequence of what I am saying is that a good instrument of Christian nurture must be designed for the continued use of the whole community, since growth, as the apostle Paul reminds us, is "measured by nothing less than the full stature of Christ." Age and intellectual development will, of course, make differences in approach and levels of presentation necessary. But the community which does not have an adequate instrument of Christian nurture for itself is in a sad way indeed. I point out that it need not be a catechism or a formal statement of faith. Who can deny that the *Book of Common Prayer* has been the real instrument of Christian nurture for the Anglicans or that for a long time the Methodist instrument of Christian nurture was a hymnbook?

If our instrument of Christian nurture serves only one segment of the community, one age level within the community, and then is forgotten, we create a spiritual vacuum which has to be filled and will, therefore, be filled with an odd assortment of things. I content myself at this point with asking whether this fact does not explain the strange conditions that are to be found within many of our Reformed and Presbyterian communities.

The Presence of God

A final word needs to be added. I was reminded of it by my reference to the Anglicans and the Methodists, though I am not sure in which category it belongs. The upbuilding of the body of Christ is not only doctrinal and personal, it is also devotional. An adequate instrument of Christian nurture should always *lead to prayer*. Please do not interpret this in a conventionally pious way. I merely want to say that from our understanding of our faith and our involvement with it there must always be a continual deepening of our sense of the presence of God in our lives. We must always be discovering how the *He* becomes *Thou*. Any instrument of Christian nurture which fails at this point has not really accomplished its task.

I hope I have sounded neither pontifical nor pedagogical; I have qualifications for neither role. I have simply been trying to say what, as a parish minister charged with the cure of souls, I am looking for in the Heidelberg Catechism as an instrument of Christian nurture.

REFORMATION CATECHISMS

When we examine the Heidelberg Catechism as to its content, we discover that by far the largest part of it is given over to questions and answers in explanation of the Apostles' Creed, the sacraments, the Ten Commandments, and the Lord's Prayer. In fact these four blocks of material account for exactly 88 of the 129 questions in the book. The fact is that the inclusion of this material for Christian instruction was common to all catechisms of the Reformation era. The catechisms of Martin Luther and John Calvin, the Prayer Book Catechism of the Anglicans, to name the most celebrated of the era, cover precisely the same blocks of material.

In selecting this particular material as basic to Christian instruction the various Reformation authors were simply following an old tradition of Western Christendom. As early as A.D. 747 the Council of Clovesho had ordered the clergy to give simple instruction in the Creed, the Lord's Prayer, the solemn words used in Holy Mass, and the sacraments themselves. Typical catechisms of the Middle Ages, such as those by Gerson or Colet, cover just these subjects, sometimes adding the Ten Commandments or the Seven Deadly Sins and the Seven Gifts of the Holy Spirit. Even in the material which they chose to cover in their catechisms the Reformers were by no means innovators but simply continued the tradition of the medieval church. It is not until the next century with the production of such manuals as the Westminster Catechisms that we find a radical departure from the traditional schema.

A comparison of these Reformation catechisms at first seems to reveal only minor differences in the order in which they treat their subjects. Luther's Small Catechism covers Law, Creed, Lord's Prayer, and two sacraments, in that order. Calvin's Catechism, the longest of any of the Reformation manuals, reverses the order of Law and Creed and, as might be supposed, entitles the last section "Word and Sacraments." The Prayer Book Catechism follows the same order as Calvin, except that the original version of 1549 did not include the section on the sacraments, which was added in 1604. The Heidelberg Catechism is essentially Calvinist in its order, the only significant difference being that the sacraments do not come at the end but between the Creed and the Law.

If we could go no further, all that we could note is that Calvin's Catechism and the Heidelberg (and whether by accident or intention, the Anglican) in their order reflect Calvin's view of the Law as an expression of gratitude and obedience and therefore as belonging in the realm of grace rather than Luther's attitude toward the Law which placed it in the old dispensation. To be sure, this is no slight difference and is fundamental to the difference between Reformed and Lutheran theology. Indeed, in a time when the Lutheran view of the Law seems to have become widely prevalent in Protestantism, another look at the Reformed view as expressed in the order of these catechisms could do no harm. But about all that can be said here is that Lutheran catechisms reflect the Lutheran stance and Reformed ones the Calvinistic stance—hardly a startling conclusion.

It is only when we begin to make comparisons in depth that the uniqueness of the Heidelberg Catechism begins to be apparent. While there is doubtless some theological reason for the order in which these subjects are treated, it would not be an exaggeration to say that in the other catechisms they are treated much as unrelated blocks of material. Slight attempts are made to connect the sections in Calvin's Catechism, for example, but they are patently artificial as witnessed by the bridge from the Law to the Lord's Prayer:

> Q. 233. Since we have spoken sufficiently of the service of God, which is the second part of his worship, let us now speak of the third part.
> A. We said it was the invocation of God in all our needs.

If I may say so, the connection between prayer and the sacraments is even more inane:

> Q. 296. It is time to come to the fourth part of the worship we render to God.
> A. We said that this consists in acknowledging with the heart and confirming with the mouth that God is the author of all good, that thereby we may glorify him.

Calvin does try to use the concept of worship, considered in four parts, as a framework in which his catechism is held. But the device fools nobody. There are four subjects to be considered and they are rather loosely strung together. (May I be permitted to add, parenthetically, that the two examples given above will serve to illustrate one of the chief reasons for the length of Calvin's Catechism—the extreme garrulousness of the questioner!)

The Catechism in Christian Nurture

A NEW APPROACH

In the case of the Heidelberg Catechism, however, we soon realize that we are dealing with a very different concept. The same elements, universally considered essential to Christian instruction, are here as in the others. But the framework in which they are set is neither accidental nor deliberately theological. I know of no better way to describe it than to say that it is biographical. To be sure there is a threefold division—man's misery, man's deliverance, man's gratitude—which at first looks as doctrinaire as Calvin's attempt to divide the material into four aspects of worship. But even the nature of this division should give us the clue that we are not in the realm of the doctrinaire. Misery, deliverance, and gratitude are not abstractions but existential realities, chapters in spiritual biography.

It has been alleged that this approach of the Heidelberg Catechism was not original but can be traced to previous Reformation documents. I am not enough of a scholar to know, though it would not surprise me if it were true. Arthur Darby Nock, my old teacher at Harvard, used to say that "originality is always the work of lost authors." But whether original or not, the Heidelberg Catechism's approach to Christian instruction makes it different from any of its contemporaries. If it were not open to misinterpretation I should be tempted to say that it interprets doctrine from the point of view of experience. I shall content myself with saying that it tells the story of the gospel from a biographical point of view.

Such an approach delivers the Heidelberger from bondage to any theological *parti pris*. Should it expound the Law from the Lutheran or the Calvinist point of view? Because Christian biography can readily recognize the validity in each (and not, I think, as is often said, because the Heidelberg Catechism was trying to find a middle way between the two theologies) our Catechism does exactly that. It would be absurd to deny that it is from the Law of God that we learn of our sin and its wretched consequences. Every Christian conscience recognizes that. So we find the Law introduced at the very beginning of the story, the schoolmaster that brings us to Christ. But it would be just as absurd for the

Christian to say that his experience of grace has removed all thought of the Law from his consciousness. He knows only too well that his joy in Christ means a life in accordance with the Law of God and for His glory. So when we come to that chapter of the story which describes the gratitude of the redeemed we find the Law again.

Such an approach also delivers the Heidelberg Catechism from tortured theological speculations in which our catechisms of a later century involved themselves. Would the man of Heidelberg have even understood what the man of Westminster was asking in his question, *"What is God?"* (I am not seeking to prove the Heidelberg Catechism a greater theological document, but only to indicate what happens when spiritual biography is forsaken for speculative theology.) Or how much would the answer: "God is a spirit, infinite, eternal, and unchangeable in his being, wisdom, power, holiness, justice, goodness, and truth" say to someone who knew this: "The eternal Father of our Lord Jesus Christ, who out of nothing created heaven and earth with all that is in them, who also upholds and governs them by his eternal counsel and providence, is for the sake of Christ his Son my God and my Father. I trust in him so completely that I have no doubt that he will provide me with all things necessary for body and soul" (Question 26)?

Or can we honestly suppose that the man of Heidelberg would not have been puzzled by the man of Westminster's anxiety about God's providence toward the angels? Or could he have possibly understood an invisible church or the speculative statement that "all who hear the gospel and live in the visible church are not saved"? Of the Holy Catholic Church he knew only that the "Son of God, by his Spirit and his Word, gathers, protects, and preserves for himself, in the unity of the true faith, a congregation chosen for eternal life. Moreover, I believe that I am and forever will remain a living member of it" (Question 54).

These comparisons (and there are many others that could be made) have been cited not for the purpose of saying that one attitude is better than another but only for the purpose of illustrating the difference between Christian instruction and Christian nurture. It is not for me to judge the fathers of Westminster.

The Catechism in Christian Nurture

But I am certain that I can say that the authors of the Heidelberg Catechism took their task of preparing an instrument for Christian nurture seriously. It would be difficult, if not impossible, to find a single question and answer in it which does not seek to relate the questioner to the doctrine under consideration, to involve him in it, to make it part of his story.

And surely this must be the reason for the Catechism's use of the first and second person singular. Its method of questioning is always to ask: "What do you believe when you say?" or "What benefit do you receive from?" Never once does it answer its questions by an abstract definition: "The meaning is . . ." or "We are to understand by this doctrine . . ." The answer is always personal: "I believe that" or "that I may be assured." Nor does the answer ever go beyond what I may experience and understand in my own person, even though the full dimensions of that experience and understanding must wait upon my growth in grace.

There have been those who have maintained that this limitation of Christian truth to what I can experience and understand puts severe limitations on its full exposition so that the Heidelberg Catechism does not present as complete a theological system as we could wish. I agree with the assertion, but I see in it a cause for rejoicing and not for complaint. First of all, I think we must be wary of "systems of doctrine" when someone tries to make them bases for Christian nurture. The very concept implies the didactic interpretation of nurture which has so plagued our Reformed tradition through the centuries.

But in the second place I think we have to remember that there is a great difference between an instrument for Christian nurture and a full confession of faith. The church has not only the right but the duty to produce this latter kind of document also. Such landmarks as the Belgic Confession, the Canons of the Synod of Dort, or the Westminster Standards testify to the fact that the Reformed churches have never shirked this duty, though one could wish that they had continued the process and that our last theological confessions, for all practical purposes, did not lie back in the seventeenth century! But we should have suffered far less from the charge of sterile didacticism if we had not confused instruments of Christian nurture with full confessions of faith, if we had remembered that the creation of a spiritual biography of necessity involves a certain amount of theological pragmatism.

A CATECHISM FOR CHRISTIANS

But I want to press further the use of the first person singular in the Heidelberg Catechism to determine who this "I" is. I think we have to read no further than the answer to Question 1 to find out: "That I belong—body and soul, in life and in death—not to myself but to my faithful Savior, Jesus Christ." Only the baptized Christian can make such a response. Only the person who stands within the covenant relationship can reply, "I belong not to myself but to my faithful Savior, Jesus Christ." In other words, this Catechism is not addressed to the pagan world, but to the Christian. It is not propaganda, but an instrument for nurture. The mere fact that it begins with the assumption that the inquirer already belongs to Jesus Christ clearly indicates that the Heidelberg Catechism is not intended for the conversion of those outside but for the upbuilding of those who are already within the redeemed community.

If it be objected that Questions 3-11 seem to have a different tone and address the inquirer as though he were a fallen son of Adam, it can be replied that this in no way changes the identity of the "I." For the remembrance of his situation apart from grace is something which certainly belongs in the spiritual biography of every Christian. And even in the biography of the baptized Christian there are chapters which, because of pride and self-will, remind him that wretchedness and misery are not homiletical exaggerations but actual descriptions of the human situation when the grace of God is no longer accepted and trusted.

THE WHOLE MAN

No, I should think that any instrument of Christian nurture which did not make us aware of this possibility would be fooling us. As it is, individually, socially, politically, internationally, yes, even ecclesiastically, we live in terms of all sorts of illusions about ourselves. It is a first obligation of genuine Christian nurture that we know what the situation really is. Only then we can begin to

The Catechism in Christian Nurture

grow into the new possibilities which grace has provided for us.

Let me also call your attention to the fact that in the Heidelberg Catechism the "I" is a total person. Again I go back to the opening answer: "I belong—*body* and soul—to Jesus Christ." I am not sure that the churches which have used the Catechism throughout these four centuries have even thought through the full implications of that opening remark. It is not a pietistic abdication of parts of human existence to other powers. There is no attempt to narrow the concern of the gospel to the need of the "soul." Here in the opening words of the Heidelberg Catechism is the frank recognition that all of human life belongs to Jesus Christ. In the deepest sense of the word what a man eats, his sexual relationships, the way he earns his living or how he pays his bills are as important to Jesus Christ as the way he says his prayers or the frequency with which he hears the domine preach.

To be sure, the fuller implications of this opening assertion are worked out later in the Catechism when we discuss our responsibility to our neighbors. And here, following Calvin's lead, the Catechism puts the Law in the context of worship and gratitude. I have always thought it significant that at that point in the liturgy where the medieval church had sung "Gloria in excelsis Deo" Calvin's little flock in Strassburg sang the Decalog. Was not Calvin trying to say here that glory to God is meaningless if it does not involve obedience and obedience meaningless if it does not involve moral character?

Because the Heidelberg Catechism does not interpret the "I" as anything less than the whole man in every aspect of his existence, it has a great ethical thrust as an instrument of Christian nurture. There is no attempt to divorce ethics from redemption. Where its point of view is taken seriously, there can be no passive acceptance of whatever takes place in government or in the social order as "none of the church's business." What would the man from Heidelberg make out of the common assertion of the *soi-disant* orthodox Reformed of today that the "church should stick to preaching the gospel and saving souls"? If I read the Catechism correctly, it would answer that we have not really preached the gospel unless the souls that have been saved have been sent out into the world with a tremendous passion to bring the total pattern of the world's existence under obedience to the kingdom of Christ.

CHRISTIAN SERVICE

The mission of the laity in the world is one of the most important elements in our present-day concept of Christian nurture. This stress that has become so significant in our time is not totally forgotten by the Heidelberg Catechism either, though tucked away in a corner waiting to be noticed. Question 86 asks about the purpose of good works. Notice the last part of its answer which gives the final and compelling reason for them: that we "by our reverent behavior may win our neighbors to Christ." Observe, in the first instance, the use of the plural pronoun. It is not my private conduct but the style of life of the entire redeemed community that is in question here. And the style of life of that community is regarded as a missionary factor of primary importance. The final reason for "good works" is not selfish and private but communal and evangelical.

An interesting study could be made of the way in which the Catechism shifts its pronouns from singular to plural, from "I" to "we." It may very well be that such a study would reveal that this shift was nothing more than chance or accident. But I cannot avoid the feeling that at many points it was a deliberate one, used to indicate that at these points we are no longer speaking about the individual, but about the Christian congregation.

Whether that be true or merely a fanciful speculation, the important point to notice is that the Heidelberg Catechism sees Christian nurture in the context of the whole Christian community. There is nothing in it to support the unchurchly evangelicalism which is so prevalent in American Protestantism or the individual development which was so characteristic of our liberalism. So far as the Catechism is concerned, acceptance of the gospel involves full participation in the life of God's holy people, the church. In its order the Heidelberg Catechism shows greater insight into the reality of Christian nurture than Calvin did. He placed "Word and Sacraments" last in his catechism, it will be remembered. The authors of the Heidelberger put them between the Creed and the Law, between the faith and its expression in life.

They put them there certainly because they recognized that without the means of grace the faith would never come to any significant expression in life. Indeed without the means of grace the faith would never gain the mastery over our existence. Question 65 is the important one in this connection:

> Q. Since, then, faith alone makes us share in Christ and all his benefits, where does such faith originate?
> A. The Holy Spirit creates it in our hearts by the preaching of the holy gospel and confirms it by the use of the holy Sacraments.

One has only to make a brief comparison of this answer with the pious vacuities about the need for faith which issue forth from our contemporary pulpits to see how seriously the Catechism takes the church as the nurturing mother, as the only context in which faith is even a possibility.

Or to look at the same question from another direction, consider where the Heidelberg Catechism locates the motivation for the Christian's life of service in the world. It comes in a place where we should hardly expect it, in the discussion in Question 103 of the meaning of the Fourth Commandment. (Notice in the answer the total absence of that fussy sabbatarianism which so bedeviled the ethics of a later Reformed tradition.)

> Q. What does God require in the fourth commandment?
> A. First, that the ministry of the gospel and Christian education be maintained, and that I diligently attend church, especially on the Lord's day, to hear the Word of God, to participate in the holy Sacraments, to call publicly upon the Lord, and to give Christian service to those in need. Second, that I cease from my evil works all the days of my life, allow the Lord to work in me through his Spirit, and thus begin in this life the eternal Sabbath.

A liturgical student like myself is interested to observe what the Catechism assumes that a Sunday service will contain—prayer, preaching, and the sacraments. But it also includes "Christian service to those in need." It includes a complete transformation of human existence in all of its relationships through the indwelling of the Spirit. In other words, the motivation for the Christian's transformed life of service in the world is located in his participation in the life of the church. And surely it is not without significance that in both cases, the appropriation of the faith and the compulsion to serve, the church is the necessary context because the church is the fellowship of the Spirit.

A CATECHISM FOR THE WHOLE CHURCH

We need to remind ourselves that it was the intention of Zacharias Ursinus and Caspar Olevianus, the authors of the Heidelberg Catechism, to provide a book for the nurture of the church and not a young people's guide to Christian theology. This is evidenced by the fact that soon after the publication of the Catechism in 1563, the same two authors prepared a simplified version of it, presumably for the instruction of children and young persons. It is further evidenced by the fact that all of the rules for its early use were for its use by the whole congregation. In the land of its birth, for example, it was divided into nine sections which were read one at a time at public worship on nine different Sundays during the year. Those of us who have a Dutch background will be more familiar with the division into fifty-two sections, commonly called "Lord's Days." The idea was that each section was to provide the basis for the preaching of one service every Sunday during the year. In fact, vestigial traces of this rule still remain in the constitution of my communion, and in the stricter Dutch churches it is still scrupulously observed.

I am not now making a brief for any particular practice. There is not one of them but can be distorted into something meaningless and artificial. What we must consider is the intention behind these rules and regulations. Does it not contain the recognition of the need for the nurture of the entire community, for its continual upbuilding in the faith, for the growth of its corporate spiritual biography? And is this not an area of badly felt need in the life of the church in our time when there is such inordinate attention given to instructing the young, retaining the interest of the adolescent, and almost none to nurturing the corporate life

The Catechism in Christian Nurture

of the Christian congregation? I personally am grateful that the Heidelberg Catechism is not only a catechism which takes the church seriously as part of the gospel, but a catechism for the edification of the body of Christ.

DEVOTIONAL QUALITY

It was no less a critic than James Moffatt who once remarked that of all the literature of the Reformation none had a more devotional quality than the Heidelberg Catechism. But does not that observation indicate a very important element of real Christian nurture? Comparisons are always odious, but let me make one anyway. Here is how three different catechisms explain the petition in the Lord's Prayer, "Thy kingdom come." Calvin takes three questions to do the job:

Q. What do you understand by the kingdom of God in the second petition?
A. It consists principally of two things: that he leads his own and governs them by his Spirit, and on the other hand casts down and confounds the reprobate who refuse to subject themselves to his rule, and so makes clear that there is no power which can resist his power.
Q. In what sense do you pray that this kingdom may come?
A. That day by day the Lord may increase the numbers of the faithful, that day by day he may increasingly bestow his graces upon them, until he has filled them completely; moreover, that he cause his truth to shine more and more and manifest his justice, so that Satan and the powers of darkness may be put to confusion and all iniquity be destroyed and abolished.
Q. Is that not taking place today?
A. Yes indeed—in part, but we pray that it may continually increase and advance, until at last it comes to its perfection in the Day of Judgment, in which God alone will be exalted, and every creature will be humbled before his majesty and he will be all in all.

The Westminster Shorter Catechism is brief and to the point:

Q. What do we pray for in the second petition?
A. In the second petition ("Thy kingdom come") we pray that Satan's kingdom may be destroyed and that the kingdom of

grace may be advanced, ourselves and others brought into it and kept in it; and that the kingdom of glory may be hastened.

This is the way the Heidelberg Catechism does it:

> Q. What is the second petition?
> A. "Thy kingdom come." That is: so govern us by thy Word and Spirit that we may more and more submit ourselves unto thee. Uphold and increase thy church. Destroy the works of the devil, every power that raises itself against thee, and all wicked schemes thought up against thy holy Word, until the full coming of thy kingdom in which thou shalt be all in all (Question 123).

The three catechisms say essentially the same thing and the dependence of the Heidelberg Catechism on Calvin is quite apparent. But what a complete difference in style and tone! The Heidelberg Catechism does not forget that devotion is also a part of nurture.

The section of the Heidelberg Catechism which deals with the Lord's Prayer is a mine of devotional treasure, for every answer, like the one quoted above, is itself a short prayer. But the devotional character of the Catechism is by no means limited to this one section. I have made a few minor changes to achieve the following:

> Eternal Father of our Lord Jesus Christ, who out of nothing created heaven and earth with all that is in them and dost uphold and govern them by thy eternal counsel and providence, we thank thee that for the sake of Christ thy Son thou art our God and our Father. Help us to trust thee so completely that we may have no doubt that thou wilt provide us with all things necessary for body and soul. Help us to know that whatever evil thou dost send upon us in this troubled life thou wilt turn to our good, even as thou art able to do it, being almighty God, and determined to do it, being a faithful Father.

You recognize, I am sure, that that prayer is only a slightly rewritten version of the answer to Question 26 which deals with the first article in the Creed: "I believe in God the Father Almighty, Maker of heaven and earth." To realize the possibilities for theological speculation or abstract discussion which such a topic contains we have only to look at the way it is treated in other catechisms. The contrast may make clear what I mean by the devotional element in Christian nurture which the Heidelberg Catechism so clearly recognizes. Nor is this by any means the only question which can so easily be made into a prayer.

Here, it seems to me, is one of the great uses of the Catechism which we almost entirely overlook. If *Lex Credendi Lex Orandi* be true, then we have an ideal instrument for its realization. Why should the Catechism not be used as devotional material in our homes along with the Bible and the Liturgy? The thoughtful consideration of a question or two every day as part of private meditation or family prayer would be a far more wholesome exercise than the reading of many of the superficial devotional guides which have gained such great popularity among our people. This is the kind of use which would bring the Catechism into greater significance as an instrument of Christian nurture, for that is its purpose.

AN INSTRUMENT FOR CHRISTIAN NURTURE

When the Heidelberg Catechism is considered and used seriously, it is an instrument for Christian nurture in depth. Here is the summary of the faith, but always presented in terms of involvement. Here is the summary of the faith, but always fostered in the context of the Christian community. Here is the summary of the faith, but relentless in its applications for our style of life in the world. Here is the summary of the faith, but one that can be said on the knees. A whole faith for a whole man for the whole of his life—and for the whole church. This is an instrument for Christian nurture. This is the Heidelberg Catechism.

Authors' Notes

CHAPTER 1

1. *Luther's Works*, 31 (Philadelphia: Muhlenberg, 1957), 39-70.
2. Luther to Spalatin, May 18, 1518. *D. Martin Luthers Briefwechsel; D. Martin Luthers Werke, kritische Gesamtausgabe*, I (Weimar, 1930 ff.), 173.
3. Hastings Eells, *Martin Bucer* (New Haven: Yale University Press, 1931), p. 4.
4. Henry Alting, *Historia Ecclesiastica Palatina* (Frankfurt, 1701), p. 143; B. G. Struve, *Ausführlicher Bericht von der Pfältzischen Kirchen-Historie* (Frankfurt, 1721), pp. 18-19.
5. See Hans Rott, *Friedrich II und die Reformation* (Heidelberg. 1904).
6. V. L. von Seckendorf, *Commentarius Historicus et Apologeticus de Lutheranismo* (Leipzig, 1694), Lib. I, sect. 57, § CLII, Additio I; Struve, *op. cit.*, p. 31.
7. See his *kirchenordnung* for Pfalz-Neuburg in A. L. Richter, ed., *Die evangelischen Kirchenordnungen des sechzehnten Jahrhunderts*, II (Leipzig: Günther, 1871), 26-30.
8. Clyde Manschreck, *Melanchthon: The Quiet Reformer* (New York and Nashville: Abingdon, 1958), ch. 2.
9. Seckendorf, *ibid.*; Struve, *op. cit.*, p. 33; Jean Sleidan, *De statu religionis et reipublicae Caroli V* (2d ed.; Strassburg, 1561), p. 477; Rott, *op. cit.*, pp. 35 f., 44 ff., 127 ff., 132 ff.; Barbara Kurze, *Kurfürst Ott Heinrich: Schriften des Vereins für Reformationsgeschichte*, Nr. 174, Jahrgang 62 (Gütersloh: Bertelsmann, 1956), pp. 15-16; Eells, *op. cit.*, p. 380.
10. Alting, *op. cit.*, p. 159; Struve, *op. cit.*, p. 37.
11. Rott, *op. cit.*, pp. 113-15.
12. B. J. Kidd, ed., *Documents Illustrative of the Continental Reformation* (Oxford: Clarendon, 1911), pp. 363-64.
13. See Kurze, *op. cit.*, pp. 53-67.
14. "Melanchthon was one of the very few who tried to bind together the segments of Reformation Christianity. . . . The title 'Father of Ecumenicity' is not inaptly applied to him." Manschreck, *op. cit.*, p. 229.
15. An excellent example of Melanchthon's reverence for tradition is found in his letter to Brenz (1535) concerning the Eucharist. *Corpus Reformatorum* 2:824. See Manschreck, *op. cit.*, p. 235.
16. *Corpus Reformatorum* 21:88.
17. See Melanchthon's correspondence on Erasmus' diatribe: *Corpus Reformatorum* 1:673, 675.
18. *Corpus Reformatorum* 21:659.
19. Chiefly Amsdorf, Flacius Illyricus, Wigand, and Hesshus. They stigmatized Melanchthon's doctrine as "synergistic." See Philip Schaff, *The Creeds of Christendom*, I (New York: Harper, 1931), 270-71.

20. See Manschreck, *op. cit.*, ch. 22 and p. 296 in particular.

21. *Corpus Reformatorum* 9:766.

22. In 1537 he wrote: "For ten years neither day nor night has passed in which I have not reflected on this subject." *Corpus Reformatorum* 3:537.

23. *Corpus Reformatorum* 1:913; 1:948.

24. "Luther's doctrine is very old in the church, and a good man will not rashly depart from the teachings of the ancients." *Corpus Reformatorum* 1:823, 830.

25. Schaff, *op. cit.*, III, 13.

26. *Corpus Reformatorum* 2:217. Oecolampadius' *Dialogus* refuted Melanchthon's own treatise in support of Luther, *Sententiae Patrum de Coena Domini. Corpus Reformatorum* 23:733-52.

27. Letter to John Brenz, January 12, 1535. *Corpus Reformatorum* 2:824.

28. See the Cassel Agreement reached by Melanchthon and Bucer in 1534: *Corpus Reformatorum* 2:808.

29. See pp. 19-20 of this book.

30. *Admonitio ultima ad Westphalum, Calvini Opera* 7:687.

31. See the *Loci* of 1559: *Corpus Reformatorum* 21:863.

32. See his *Examen Ordinandorum: Corpus Reformatorum* 23:62.

33. Cited by Struve, *op. cit.*, p. 51.

34. Cited in Carl Schmidt, *Philipp Melanchthon* (Elberfeld, 1861), p. 371.

35. Letter to Veit Dietrich, 1538. *Corpus Reformatorum* 3:514.

36. *Ibid.*

37. See the Cassel Agreement with Bucer: *Corpus Reformatorum* 2:808. See also the *Wittenberg Concord: Corpus Reformatorum* 3:75 ff.

38. *Corpus Reformatorum* 2:861, 871; 3:180; 4:34, 37.

39. Schaff, *ibid.*; H. E. Jacobs, ed., *The Book of Concord*, II (Philadelphia: Frederick, 1893), 109.

40. Jacobs, *ibid.*, 112.

41. Manschreck, *op. cit.*, pp. 247, 299, 301.

42. *Corpus Reformatorum*, 5:474, 476, 478. See Manschreck, *op. cit.*, pp. 242-47.

43. Jacobs, *op. cit.*, I, 11.

44. See Manschreck, *op. cit.*, ch. 21.

45. *John Calvin's Tracts and Treatises*, II (Grand Rapids: Eerdmans, 1958), 355-56.

46. Alting, *op. cit.*, p. 161; Struve, *op. cit.*, p. 52.

47. Kurze, *op. cit.*, pp. 67-68.

48. Richter, *op. cit.*, II, 131-41, 146, 177-78.

49. See Kurze, *op. cit.*, pp. 53-54, 56.

50. Richter, *op. cit.*, II, 137.

51. Struve, *op. cit.*, p. 48.

52. *Corpus Reformatorum* 23: xxxv-cx (German); 23:1-102 (Latin).

53. See Luther D. Reed, *The Lutheran Liturgy* (Philadelphia: Muhlenberg, 1947), p. 89.

54. Richter, *op. cit.*, II, 138-39.

55. Alting, *op. cit.*, p. 165; Struve, *op. cit.*, p. 52; Kurze, *op. cit.*, p. 70.

56. On the reorganization of the ministry, see Struve, *op. cit.*, p. 52; Alting, *op. cit.*, p. 163.

57. Ludwig Häusser, *Geschichte der Rheinische Pfalz*, I (1844), 635; Kurze, *op. cit.*, p. 73.

58. Struve, *op. cit.*, p. 53.

59. On Melanchthon's visit, see *Corpus Reformatorum* 9:341, 343; J. W. Richard, *Philip Melanchthon* (New York: Putnam, 1898), p. 370. On the importance of Melanchthon's advice, see Joachim Came-

rarii, *De Vita Melanchthonis Narratio*, p. 371; Walther Köhler, "Philipp Melanchthon und die Reform der Universität Heidelberg 1557" in *Neue Heidelberger Jahrbücher*, 1937.

60. *Kurfürst Ott Heinrich*, pp. 68-69.

61. See Struve, *op. cit.*, p. 54.

62. *John Calvin's Tracts and Treatises*, II, 503.

63. See "Clear Explanation of Sound Doctrine Concerning the True Partaking of the Flesh and Blood of Christ in the Holy Supper, in Order to Dissipate the Mists of Tileman Heshusius," *John Calvin's Tracts and Treatises*, II, 495-572 (and 573-79).

64. In the 1560's Erastus defended the Zwinglian view in a book, *Vom Verstand der Wort Christi: Das ist mein Leib*. See "Erastus," in *The New Schaff-Herzog Religious Encyclopedia*, IV (1909), 167-68. See also R. Wesel-Roth, *Thomas Erastus* (1954).

65. Rott, "Ottheinrich und die Kunst" in *Mitteilungen des Heidelberger Schlossvereins*, V (1910), 124 ff.

66. Struve, *op. cit.*, pp. 66-67; Alting, *op. cit.*, pp. 168-69.

67. Struve, *op. cit.*, p. 66.

68. *Ibid.*, p. 76.

69. Melanchthon expressed his alarm over this situation in letters to Brenz and Bucer of April 21, 1557. *Corpus Reformatorum* 9:144, 146.

70. See August Kluckhohn, *Die Briefe Kurfürst Friedrichs des Frommen von der Pfalz*, Vol. I (1559-1566), Vol. II/1 (1567-1572), Vol. II/2 (1572-1576). Braunschweig: Schwetschke, 1868-72. See also Kluckhohn, *Kurfürst Friedrich der Fromme* (Nördlingen, 1877-79); Walter Hollweg, *Neue Untersuchungen zur Geschichte und Lehre des Heidelberger Katechismus* (Neukirchen, 1961), ch. 1, "Friedrich III, der Fromme, Kurfürst von der Pfalz: Der Mensch—Der Christ."

71. The theses are given in Struve, *op. cit.*, p. 78.

72. *Ibid.*, p. 80.

73. *Ibid.*, pp. 81-82.

74. Cited in James I. Good, *The Heidelberg Catechism in Its Newest Light* (Philadelphia, 1914), p. 141.

75. *Responsio Philip. Melanth. ad quaestionem de controversia Heidelbergensi*. *Corpus Reformatorum* 9:960-62.

76. See Struve, *op. cit.*, p. 87.

77. *Ibid.*

78. See his negotiations with John à Lasco (1556) in A. Kuyper, ed., *Joannis a Lasco Opera*, II (Amsterdam: Muller, 1866), 724-30.

79. Heinrich Heppe, *Die Entstehung und Fortbildung des Lutherthums und die kirchlichen Bekenntnisschriften desselben von 1548-1576* (Cassel: Fischer, 1863), pp. 60 ff.

80. Schaff, *op. cit.*, I, 290-93.

81. *Corpus Reformatorum* 9:1036.

82. See "Stoessel" in *The New Schaff-Herzog Religious Encyclopedia*, XI (1911), 100-1.

83. For text see Struve, *op. cit.*, p. 98.

84. For complete text see *ibid.*, pp. 94-98.

85. Many of the older historians declare flatly (and I would say, erroneously) that Frederick was "converted to Calvinism" then and there. See Good, *op. cit.*, p. 153; Alting, *op. cit.*, pp. 182 ff.; Struve, *op. cit.*, pp. 103-6. Kluckhohn is more cautious; see *Kurfürst Friedrich der Fromme*, p. 73.

86. See "Naumburg" in *The New Schaff-Herzog Religious Encyclopedia*, VIII (1910), 87.

87. Kluckhohn, *Briefe*, I, 158 ff.

88. The preface to the *Naumburg Repetition* (February 1, 1561) recognized the *Variata* as "the same Confession, repeated in a somewhat more stately and elaborate manner, and also explained and enlarged on the basis of holy scripture." It also admitted that "that clarified Confession, which was published in the years 1540 and 1542, is to a much greater degree in use in our churches and schools." Heppe, *Die Bekenntnisschriften der altprotestantischen Kirche Deutschlands* (Cassel: Fischer, 1855), pp. 583-97.

89. Kluckhohn, *Briefe*, I, 662. Many other examples will be cited below.

90. See Karl Sudhoff, *C. Olevianus und Z. Ursinus: Leben und ausgewählte Schriften* (Elberfeld: Friederich, 1857); Julius Ney, *Die Reformation in Trier, 1559* (Halle, 1906-07).

91. *The New Schaff-Herzog Religious Encyclopedia*, III (1909), 358-59.

92. *Ibid.*, XI (1911), 504.

93. Struve, *op. cit.*, p. 106; Alting, *op. cit.*, pp. 183-84.

94. Cited in J. C. McLelland, *The Visible Words of God: An Exposition of the Sacramental Theology of Peter Martyr Vermigli A.D. 1500-1562* (Edinburgh: Oliver & Boyd, 1957), p. x.

95. Ursinus to Crato von Crafftheim, 1557. Sudhoff, *op. cit.*, p. 487. See J. F. A. Gillet, *Crato von Crafftheim und seine Freunde*, 2 vols. (Frankfurt, 1860).

96. This assumption rests chiefly on Ursinus' inaugural address at Breslau, to which I do not have access. See Sudhoff, *op. cit.*, p. 4; Good, *op. cit.*, p. 249.

97. *Theses complectentes breviter et perspicue summam verae Doctrinae de Sacramentis etc.* Quirinus Reuter, ed., *Ursini Opera*, I, 755-803.

98. Sudhoff, *op. cit.*, p. 5.

99. For text see *ibid*, p. 9.

100. Wilhelm Niesel, ed., *Bekenntnisschriften und Kirchenordnungen der nach Gottes Wort reformierten Kirche* (Zurich: Evangelishcher Verlag, 1938), pp. 138-39.

101. See Walter Hollweg, *op. cit.*; Good, *op. cit.*; M. A. Gooszen, *De Heidelbergsche Catechismus* (Leiden, 1890); August Lang, *Der Heidelberger Katechismus und vier verwandte Katechismen* (Leipzig, 1907).

102. See Struve, *op. cit.*, pp. 139 ff.

103. Niesel, *op. cit.*, p. 139. In the prolegomena of his *Commentary* on the Catechism, Ursinus also declared that the work was committed "to certain devout men famous for their erudition in Christian doctrine."

104. Olevianus mentioned the work of Erastus in a letter to Calvin, April 14, 1563. Sudhoff, *op. cit.*, pp. 482-83.

105. Stephen Zierler (Cirler), the Elector's secretary. Barbara Kurze counts him among the Zwinglians: *Kurfürst Ott Heinrich*, p. 70.

106. Kluckhohn, *Briefe*, I, 726: "I can prove by my own handwriting that, having received my catechism from my theologians, and having read it, I corrected it in several places."

107. See Heinrich Simon van Alpen, *The History and Literature of the Heidelberg Catechism*, tr. by J. F. Berg (Philadelphia: Martien, 1863), p. 23.

108. Hollweg, *op. cit.*, ch. 3.

109. Niesel, *op. cit.*, p. 139. See also the Palatinate Consistorial

Order of 1564 in Richter, *op. cit.*, II, 277.

110. See Olevianus' letter to Calvin, April 3, 1563: *Corpus Reformatorum* 19:683-85.

111. The date of the Elector's preface to the whole Church Order. Niesel, *op. cit.*, p. 141.

112. Letter of October 25, 1563. Sudhoff, *op. cit.*, pp. 483-85.

113. Kuyper, *op. cit.*, 45-262.

114. Niesel, *op. cit.*, p. 187.

115. Kluckhohn, *Briefe,* I, 398.

116. *Ibid.,* 399.

117. *Ibid.,* 449-60.

118. *Ibid.,* 461.

119. *Ibid.,* 464 ff.

120. *Ibid.,* 504-5. See also Schaff, *op. cit.*, I, 288-89.

121. Kluckhohn, *Briefe,* I, 661-64; Struve, *op. cit.*, 187-90.

122. Kluckhohn, *Briefe,* I, 622.

123. *Ibid.,* 677-82.

124. See Frederick's letter to Bullinger, May 19, 1566 in Kluckhohn, *Briefe,* II/2, 1039-40.

125. Kluckhohn, *Briefe,* I, 726.

126. In particular, see *Gründlicher Bericht vom h. Abendmahl unsers Herrn Jesu Christ, aus einhelliger Lehre, der heiligen Schrift, der alten rechtgläubigen Christlichen Kirchen, und auch der Augspurgischen Confession. . . . Auch Herrn Philippi Melanchthonis Bedencken über der spaltung vom Abendmahl... MDLXXIV.* This work, in which Melanchthon's *Responsio* was appended, is quoted at large in A. Ebrard, *Das Dogma vom heiligen Abendmahl,* II (Frankfurt, 1845), 618-34. See also *Augspurgischer Confession, derselben Apologia, und Repetition; auch Frankfordischen abschieds lere von Sacramenten* (Heidelberg, 1566). This catechetical aid is reproduced in Heppe, *Die confessionelle Entwicklung der alt-protestantischen Kirche Deutschlands* (Marburg: Elwert, 1854).

127. Heppe, *Die Bekenntnisschriften der reformirten Kirchen Deutschlands* (Elberfeld, 1860), pp. 1-18. The text is also in Struve, *op. cit.,* pp. 275-92.

128. Schaff, *op. cit.*, I, 549.

CHAPTER 2

1. See James E. Sellers, "The Church and Mass Communication," unpublished Ph.D. dissertation (Vanderbilt University, 1958).

2. See Luther's preface to his *Large Catechism:* H. E. Jacobs, ed., *The Book of Concord,* I (Philadelphia: Frederick, 1893), 383-87.

3. *Luther's Works,* 13 (St. Louis: Concordia, 1956), 386.

4. See Luther's sermon on the Sermon on the Mount. *Luther's Works,* 21 (St. Louis: Concordia, 1956), 34-35.

5. *Sermon on 1 Timothy,* 3:8-10. *Corpus Reformatorum* 53:300.

6. *Commentary on Acts,* 8:31. *Corpus Reformatorum* 48:191-92.

7. See *Institutes* 4:14:8. See also *Commentary on 2 Corinthians,* 1:24: *Corpus Reformatorum* 50:26.

8. See Luther's preface to his *Small Catechism:* Jacobs, *op. cit.*, 360.

9. "On the Councils and the Churches." *Works of Martin Luther,* V (Philadelphia: Holman, 1931). 270-71.

10. See *Articles Concerning the Organization of the Church and of Worship at Geneva, 1537. Library of Christian Classics,* XXII (Philadelphia: Westminster, 1954), 54. See also *Draft Ecclesiastical Ordinances. Library of Christian Classics,* XXII, 69.

11. *Library of Christian Classics,* XXII, 88.

12. See Frederick Eby, *Early Protestant Educators*, p. 97.
13. Jacobs, *op. cit.*, 364.
14. *Corpus Reformatorum* 8:412.
15. *Institutes* 4:1:4.
16. A. L. Richter, ed., *Die evangelischen Kirchenordnungen des sechszehnten Jahrhunderts*, II (Leipzig: Günther, 1871), 277.
17. See *Commentary on Ephesians*, 4:11. See also *Institutes* 4:1:5.
18. See Richter, *op. cit.*, 277 f.
19. *Institutes* 4:3:6.
20. See "The Adultero—German Interim." *John Calvin's Tracts and Treatises*, III (Grand Rapids: Eerdmans, 1958), 207. See also *Tracts*, III, 366-67.
21. *Commentary on Ephesians*, 4:11.
22. Cf. R. H. Wallace, *Calvin's Doctrine of the Word and Sacrament* (Edinburgh: Oliver & Boyd, 1958), p. 115.
23. See *Institutes* 4:1:5; 4:17:25.
24. *Commentary on 2 Timothy*, 2:15. *Commentary on Daniel*, 7:15.
25. *Commentary on Ephesians*, 4:12; the final sentence has been relocated.
26. "On Shunning the Unlawful Rites of the Ungodly." *John Calvin's Tracts and Treatises*, III, 366-67.
27. *Institutes* 4:3:16.
28. *Commentary on Isaiah*, 61:1.
29. "Acts of the Council of Trent with the Antidote." *John Calvin's Tracts and Treatises*, III, p. 177.
30. *The Commentary of Dr. Zacharias Ursinus on the Heidelberg Catechism* (Columbus: Scott & Bascom, 1852), p. 446.
31. Namely the translation of G. W. Williard, 1851.
32. The Latin is: "Quia usu legitimo est coniuncta exhibitio et perceptio signorum et rerum." See *Corpus doctrinae Orthodoxae sive Catecheticarum explicationum D. Zachariae Ursini* (Heidelberg, 1612), p. 423.
33. *Ibid.*, p. 412.
34. Ursinus treats this problem on pp. 423-30 of *Corpus doctrinae Orthodoxae*.
35. *Commentary on Acts*, 3:25. See *Institutes* 4:16.
36. *Institutes* 4:16:7.
37. Wilhelm Niesel, ed., *Bekenntnisschriften und Kirchenordnungen der nach Gottes Wort reformierten Kirche* (Zurich: Evangelischer Verlag, 1938), pp. 143-48; especially p. 147.
38. *Ibid.*, pp. 187-88 (Rubrics for the Preparatory Service).
39. *Corpus doctrinae Orthodoxae*, p. 429.
40. Niesel, *op. cit.*, pp. 143, 148.
41. *Ibid.*, p. 187.
42. *Institutes*, 4:17:32.
43. Quoted by J. S. Whale in *The Protestant Tradition* (Cambridge University Press, 1959), p. 57.
44. *Articles of 1537*. Library of Christian Classics, XXII, 50.
45. *Ibid.*, p. 49.
46. *Institutes* 4:12.
47. *Corpus doctrinae Orthodoxae*, pp. 491-528.
48. *Institutes* 4:12:1.
49. *Corpus Reformatorum* 1:72-74.
50. *Corpus Reformatorum* 1:74.
51. Whale, *op. cit.*, p. 146. I am especially indebted to Whale throughout this section.
52. *Institutes* 4:1:4.
53. *Institutes* 4:1:1.
54. A new translation of the Palatinate Liturgy, by Bard Thompson, is found in *Theology and Life* 6/1 (Spring, 1963), 49-67.
55. *Institutes* 4:18:20.
56. *Institutes* 3:4:10 f.
57. *Institutes* 3:4:12 ff.

58. Edition 1536. See Richter, *op. cit.*, I, 268.
59. The *Book of Worship* (Evangelical and Reformed) reads: "Hearken now unto the comforting assurance of the grace of God, promised in the gospel to all that repent and believe."
60. In the Palatinate Liturgy, a collect for illumination is appended to the opening prayer of confession.
61. *Commentary on Psalm* 106.
62. *Commentary on 1 Peter*, 1:25.
63. *Institutes* 4:17:39.
64. *Library of Christian Classics*, XXII, p. 137.
65. *Theology and Life*, 6/1 (Spring, 1963), 65.
66. John W. Nevin, *The Mystical Presence* (Philadelphia: Fisher, 1867), p. 59.
67. *John Calvin's Tracts and Treatises*, III, 281.
68. See Wallace, *op. cit.*, ch. XIII.
69. Whale, *op. cit.*, p. 133. Italics are mine.
70. From the liturgical *Schema* of Vatican II.

CHAPTER 3

1. *The Proceedings of the Synod of the German Reformed Church* at York Pa., September, 1827 (Hagerstown, Md., 1828), p. 25.
2. These several matters are discussed in David Dunn, et al., *A History of the Evangelical and Reformed Church* (Philadelphia: The Christian Education Press, 1961), ch. 3.
3. *Memoirs of the Rev. Charles G. Finney*, written by himself (New York: Barnes, 1876), p. 189.
4. *Ibid.*, pp. 238-55.
5. *The Magazine of the German Reformed Church*, II (1829), 159.
6. *The Acts and Proceedings of the Synod of the German Reformed Church* at Reading, Pa., October 1841 (Chambersburg, Pa., 1841), p. 26.
7. *The Acts and Proceedings of the Synod of the German Reformed Church* at Allentown, Lehigh Co., Pa., 1844 (Chambersburg, 1844), p. 28.
8. *The Messenger*, Dec. 16, 1840, p. 1092.
9. *A Sermon Delivered at the Opening of the Synod at Reading, Pa.*, October 21, 1841 (Chambersburg, 1841), p. 4. Appended to *The Acts and Proceedings* of 1841.
10. See John W. Nevin, *The Anxious Bench* (Chambersburg, 1844), p. 119.
11. These details are given in J. H. A. Bomberger, *The Revised Liturgy* (Philadelphia, 1867), pp. 13 ff.
12. Theodore Appel, *Recollections of College Life at Marshall College* (Reading: Miller, 1886), pp. 165-67.
13. *Liturgy for the Use of the Congregations of the German Reformed Church. Approved by the Synod of said church.* (Chambersburg, 1841.)
14. *The Messenger*, Jan. 27, 1841.
15. See *The Messenger*, Nov. 11, 1840; Sept. 15, 1841; July 13, 1842.
16. *Liturgy for the Use of the Congregations of the German Reformed Church*, pp. 53 ff.
17. *The Acts and Proceedings of the Synod of the German Reformed Church* at Greencastle, Pa., October, 1840 (Chambersburg, 1840), p. 26.
18. *A Sermon Delivered at the Opening of the Synod at Reading, Pa.*, October 21, 1841 (Chambersburg, 1841), pp. 7, 10.
19. *The Acts and Proceedings of the Synod of the German Reformed*

Church at Allentown, Lehigh Co., Pa., 1844, p. 34.
20. *The Acts and Proceedings of the Synod of the German Reformed Church* at Greencastle, Pa., October, 1840 (Chambersburg, 1840), pp. 76 ff.
21. See *The Messenger*, Feb. 2, 1842; June 29, 1842.
22. *A Sermon Delivered at the Opening of the Synod at Reading, Pa.*, p. 10.
23. In his famous sermon at the opening of the Synod of 1844. See *The Messenger*, Nov. 20, 1844, p. 1913.
24. *The Messenger*, Nov. 25, 1840, p. 1079.
25. Jan. 12, p. 1315; Feb. 2, p. 1324; Feb. 16, p. 1334.
26. *Addresses Delivered at the Inauguration of the Rev. J. W. Nevin, D.D.* (Chambersburg, 1840), p. 24.
27. Notice the examples in *The Anxious Bench*.
28. See John Willison, *A Sacramental Catechism* (revised edition; Pittsburgh: Loomis, 1830). This catechism subscribed to Calvin's doctrine of the Eucharist. Nevin's endorsement of the catechism is printed on p. iv.
29. See "The Heidelberg Catechism," *The Messenger*, Aug. 10, 1842, p. 1433. See also Nevin's defense of the revival at Reading: *The Messenger*, June 14, 1843, p. 1612.
30. Jan. 27, 1841, p. 1012.
31. Apr. 27, 1842, p. 1373.
32. *The Anxious Bench* (2d ed., revised and enlarged; Chambersburg, 1844).
33. Bound with Philip Schaff, *The Principle of Protestantism* (Chambersburg, 1845), pp. 191-215.
34. *The Anxious Bench* (1844), pp. 124-25.
35. "Catholic Unity," p. 195.
36. *The Anxious Bench* (1844), p. 130.
37. *Ibid.*, pp. 128-29.
38. "Catholic Unity," pp. 201-2.
39. *Ibid.*, p. 203.
40. See note 23.
41. Expanded for publication as (1) *The Principle of Protestantism*, translated from the German with an introduction by J. W. Nevin (Chambersburg, 1845); (2) *Das Princip des Protestantismus*, (Chambersburg, 1845).
42. Schaff, *op. cit.*, p. 49.
43. A full and fair estimate of this matter is given in James H. Nichols, *Romanticism in American Theology* (University of Chicago Press, 1961), ch. 5. Schaff himself wrote: "We wish not to endorse Hegel's theology of development without qualification; but whatever may be thought of it, one thing is certain. It has left an impression on German science that can never be effaced; and has contributed more than any other influence to diffuse a clear conception of the interior organism of history, as a richer evolution continually of the idea of humanity, as well as a proper respect for its universal and objective authority, in opposition to the self-sufficient and arrogant individualism of the rationalistic school. . . . Here, however, we come also on the fatal rock of this speculative [Hegelian] method of history. While Rationalism had scarcely the most remote conception of a divine presence in history, and resolved everything into free human activity, the philosophy before us falls over to the opposite extreme of pantheism and fatalism. . . . The Hegelian philosophy then is in itself no safe conductor through the halls of church history. . . . Whilst it has led the way for many to a historical and

churchly spirit, and proved an admirable help toward the overthrow of the common Rationalism, and a thorough speculative understanding and defense of Orthodoxy; it has served, on the other hand, when sundered from the real life-revelation of Christianity, to produce itself a new form of Rationalism, very different from the first—more spiritual indeed—but for this reason also more dangerous, that from an opposite direction shows the most radical hostility to all concrete and individual historical life." Schaff, *What Is Church History?* (Philadelphia: Lippincott, 1846), pp. 75-77.

44. Schaff, *The Principle of Protestantism*, p. 51.

45. See Schaff, *What Is Church History?* Pp. 82 ff.

46. Schaff, *The Principle of Protestantism*, p. 52.

47. *Ibid.*, pp. 47-50.

48. *Ibid.*, p. 146; see also pp. 146-176.

49. *Ibid.*, pp. 169, 173.

50. *Ibid.*, p. 174.

51. *Ibid.*, pp. 175-76.

52. *Ibid.*, p. 173.

53. Joseph F. Berg, *The Old Paths, or a Sketch of the Order and Discipline of the Reformed Church Before the Reformation, as Maintained by the Waldenses Prior to That Epoch, and by the Church of the Palatinate in the 16th Century* (Philadelphia: Lippincott, 1845).

54. The controversy provoked by the early writings of Nevin and Schaff is discussed in James I. Good, *History of the Reformed Church in the U.S. in the Nineteenth Century* (New York, 1911), pp. 219-30.

55. See Schaff, *What Is Church History?* P. 71.

56. *The Acts and Proceedings of the Synod of the German Reformed Church* at York, York Co., Pa., October, 1845 (Chambersburg, 1845), pp. 74-75.

57. *Ibid.*, pp. 73-91.

58. Nevin, *The Mystical Presence* (Philadelphia: Fisher, 1867), pp. 3-6.

59. *Ibid.*, p. 63.

60. *Ibid.*, p. 67.

61. *Ibid.*, pp. 88 ff.

62. *Ibid.*, pp. 54-55, 164-77.

63. See *ibid.*, pp. 156-63.

64. *Ibid.*, pp. 61, 183 f.

65. Nevin, "Doctrine of the Reformed Church on the Lord's Supper," *The Mercersburg Review*, II (1850), 421-548.

66. *Ibid.*, p. 523.

67. *Ibid.*, pp. 521, 523.

68. *Ibid.*, pp. 524, 526.

69. *Ibid.*, p. 523.

70. Nichols, *op. cit.*, p. 106.

71. *Pulpit and Table* (Richmond: John Knox, 1962), p. 97.

72. Chambersburg: Publication Office of the German Reformed Church, 1847.

73. IX, "Theology of the Catechism," 125-39.

74. X, "Church Spirit of the Catechism," 139-62.

75. *Ibid.*, p. 154.

76. *Ibid.*, pp. 156, 161.

77. *The Acts and Proceedings of the Synod of the German Reformed Church* at Lancaster, Pa., October 14, 1847 (Chambersburg, 1848), p. 23.

78. *The Acts and Proceedings of the Synod of the German Reformed Church* at Hagerstown, Md., October, 1848 (Chambersburg, 1848), pp. 74-75.

79. *The Acts and Proceedings of the Synod of the German Reformed Church* at Norristown, Pa., October, 1849 (Chambersburg, 1849), pp. 79-82.

80. Schaff, "The New Liturgy," *The Mercersburg Review*, X (1858), 208-9.

81. *The Messenger*, March 29, 1848.
82. See Schaff, *The Principle of Protestantism*, p. 148.
83. Schaff, "The New Liturgy," 202-17.
84. *Ibid.*, pp. 217-20.
85. *The Acts and Proceedings of the Synod of the German Reformed Church* at Baltimore, Md., October, 1852 (Chambersburg, 1852), p. 85.
86. In his introduction to *The Principle of Protestantism*, p. 8.
87. "Catholic Unity," p. 214.
88. Schaff, *The Principle of Protestantism*, p. 128.
89. *Ibid.*, pp. 160-61.

CHAPTER 4

1. For the Latin text see August Lang, *Der Heidelberger Katechismus und vier verwandte Katechismen* (Leipzig, 1907), p. 152.
2. *Ibid.*, p. 200.
3. *Ibid.*
4. For the Latin see Henrici Altingii, "Historia Ecclesiastica Palatina" in Friderici Sylburgii, *Catalogus* (Frankfurt, 1701), p. 189.
5. For the German see Wilhelm Niesel, ed., *Bekenntnisschriften und Kirchenordnungen der nach Gottes Wort reformierten Kirche*, (Munich, 1938), p. 139.
6. M. A. Gooszen, *De Heidelbergsche Catechismus* (Leiden, 1890), pp. 1-30.
7. See August Kluckhohn, *Die Briefe Kurfürst Friedrichs des Frommen von der Pfalz*, I (Braunschweig, 1868), 310 f. The letter is directed to his son-in-law, Duke John Frederick of Saxony.
8. For the German see Niesel, *op. cit.*, p. 139.
9. For the Latin see Alting, *op. cit.*, pp. 189 f.
10. See Otto Thelemann, *Handreichung zum Heidelberger Katechismus* (2d ed.; Detmold, 1892), pp. 515 f.
11. See Niesel, *op. cit.*, p. 140.
12. The Latin original of most of this passage is found in Heinrich Ott, *Dogmatik und Verkündigung* (Zurich, 1961), p. 27.
13. For the Latin see Alting, *op. cit.*, p. 189.
14. Philip Schaff, "Geschichte, Geist und Bedeutung des Heidelberger Katechismus: Ein Beitrag zur dreihundertjährigen Jubelfeier" in *Zeitschrift für die historische Theologie*, III (1864), 355.
15. See Walter Hollweg, *Neue Untersuchungen zur Geschichte und Lehre des Heidelberger Katechismus* (Neukirchen, 1961), pp. 86-123.
16. See the books by Gooszen and Lang already quoted and James I. Good, *The Heidelberg Catechism in Its Newest Light* (Philadelphia, 1914). Gooszen gives a synopsis of the Heidelberg Catechism with some other catechisms.
17. Letter of May 11, 1560. *Corpus Reformatorum* 18:84.
18. For the German see Schaff, *op. cit.*, 328.
19. George W. Richards, *The Heidelberg Catechism* (Philadelphia, 1913), p. 96.
20. For the German see Lang, *op. cit.*, pp. 103 f. One should note that the word ecumenical was highly unusual in 1907!

CHAPTER 5

1. See Karl Barth, *Kirchliche Dogmatik*, I, 2, 9-11; Barth, *Die christliche Lehre nach dem Heidelberger Katechismus*, pp. 42 f.
2. Barth, *Kirchliche Dogmatik*, I, 2, 11.
3. Paul Jacobs, *Theologie refor-*

mierter Bekenntnisschriften (Neukirchen, 1959), p. 67.
4. G. C. Berkouwer, *Het werk van Christus* (Kampen, 1953), p. 257.
5. Barth, *Die christliche Lehre nach dem Heidelberger Katechismus*, pp. 70, 72.
6. Barth, *Kirchliche Dogmatik*, II, 1, 551.
7. Compare the felicitous expression in the *Statement of Faith* of the United Church of Christ: "He calls us into his Church to accept the *cost* and *joy* of discipleship."
8. Barth, *Kirchliche Dogmatik*, IV, 2, 650 ff.

CHAPTER 6

1. W. Kramer, *Christos—Kyrios—Gottessohn* (Zurich, 1963). Cf. also the outstanding dissertation of Ferdinand Hahn, *Anfänge christologischer Traditionen im Neuen Testament* (Göttingen, 1963).
2. Cf., for instance, Eduard Schweizer, *Spirit of God* (London, 1960), pp. 57 f.
3. "Es ist das eine Taklosigkeit von welthistorischen Dimensionen, der grösste Exzess der falschen Stellung, die sich Lukas zum Gegenstand gibt. . . . Lukas behandelt historiographisch, was keine Geschichte und auch so nicht überliefert war." F. Overbeck, *Christentum und Kultur* (1919), pp. 78 f.
4. Cf. Schweizer, *Orthodox Proclamation, Interpretation 1954*, pp. 387 ff.
5. Cf. Hahn, *op. cit.*
6. Cf. K. Aland, "Das Problem des neutestamentlichen Kanons" in *Neue Zeitschrift für systematische Theologie* (April 1962), pp. 220-42, and the literature mentioned there.
7. Cf. Schweizer, *Church Order in the New Testament* (London, 1961). Cf. also Schweizer, "Unity and Diversity in the New Testament Teaching Regarding the Church," in *Theology Today*, (XIII, 1956/57), 471 ff.
8. Cf. E. Käsemann, "Begründet der neutestamentliche Kanon die Einheit der Kirche?" in *Exegetische Versuche und Besinnungen* (Göttingen, 1960) pp. 214-23.
9. An English translation of the so-called "Arnoldshainer Thesen" is to be found in G. Niemeier, ed., *Lehrgespräch über das Heilige Abendmahl* (Munich, 1961), pp. 332-34.
10. Cf. Schweizer, *Spirit of God*, pp. 45 f., 67 ff., 91 ff.
11. Cf. Schweizer in *Current Issues in New Testament Interpretation: Essays in Honor of Otto A. Piper* (New York, 1962), pp. 166-77; also in *Neotestamentica*, German and English Essays (Zurich: Zwingli Verlag, 1963).
12. Gregory Dix, *Jew and Greek* (New York: Harper & Row, 1953), p. 80 f.
13. Cf., for instance, J. Jeremias, "Kennzeichen der ipsissima vox Jesu," in *Synoptische Studien: A. Wikenhauser-Festschrift* (Munich, 1954), pp. 86-93; J. M. Robinson, *A New Quest of the Historical Jesus* (London, 1959); and G. Ebeling, *Theologie und Verkündigung* (Tübingen, 1962).
14. Cf. Schweizer in *Neotestamentica et Patristica: Freundesgabe für Oscar Cullmann* (Leiden, 1962), pp. 35-46. Cf. note 11.
15. Cf. Schweizer, "The Disciples of Jesus and the Post-resurrection Church," *Union Seminary Quarterly Review* (No. 15, 1960), pp. 281-94. Cf. note 11.
16. Recently again in Rudolf Bultmann, *Das Verhältnis der urchristlichen Christusbotschaft zum*

historischen Jesus (SAH, Heidelberg, 1960).

CHAPTER 7

1. Cf. Eduard Schweizer, *Spirit of God* (London, 1960); *The Spirit of Power, Interpretation* 6 (1952), pp. 259-78; *The Service of Worship, an Exposition of 1 Corinthians 14, Interpretation* 13 (1959), pp. 400-8.
2. Cf. J. M. Robinson, *A New Quest of the Historical Jesus* (London, 1959).
3. Cf. Rudolf Bultmann, *Das Verhältnis der urchristlichen Christusbotschaft zum historischen Jesus* (SAH, Heidelberg, 1960), pp. 8 f.
4. Cf. H. Graffmann in *Die Religion in Geschichte und Gegenwart*, III (3d ed.; Tübingen, 1959), 127 f.
5. Cf. J. Jeremias, *Unbekannte Jesusworte*, (3d ed.; 1962).

CHAPTER 8

1. J. D. Benoit, "Les Déficits de la Predication" (an address delivered at the Synod of the Reformed Church of Alsace-Lorraine, September 1952), pp. 4-5.

www.ingramcontent.com/pod-product-compliance
Lightning Source LLC
Chambersburg PA
CBHW071423160426

43195CB00013B/1791